D1245895

Only Through The Will Of God   Shall Our Freedom Be Preserved

The
Double Gun
Journal

Fall Flight

1929 Watercolour
by W.J. Schaldach

IN APPRECIATION

Wm. O. Achtermeier	Bernard H. DiGiacobbe, M.D.	Catherine Harper	Worth & Marge Mathewson	W. C. Snyder
Terry Allen	Chris Dorsey	William W. Headrick	Peter Matthias	Dale Spartas
Tom Archer	Spence Dupree	Stephen C. Helsley	John F. Milius	Jeff Stephens
David J. Baker	Robert I. Egbert	John Houchins	Dr. Martin Moog	Håkan Stenlund
Larry Barnes	James E. Fender	Andrew Iosson	Ed Muderlak	John Tassini
Sherman Bell	Bill Ferguson	Tony Jackson	Ray & Jeanette Mudge	John Taylor
Mark K. Benenson	Frank Findlow	Ivan Johnson	Wm. L. Mullins	David Adams Thompson
Steve Bodio	Fredrik Franzén	Keith Kearcher	Gary Murphy	David Trevallion
Geoffrey Boothroyd	Adam Freeman	Tom Kidd	Felix Neuberger	David Truesdale
John Brindle	Les Freer	Philip Kroll	Jan Nilsson	James T. Tyson
Col. Wm. S. Brophy	William M. Furnish	Roger Lake	Bob Noble	Edward E. Ulrich
Larry Brown	Oscar Gaddy	Randy E. Lawrence	David J. Noreen	Joseph T. Vorisek
Paul Brown	Miles Gilbert	Ira Lewis	John Ormiston	Stan Warren
Eldon Buckner	Martin Godio	Keith McCafferty	Roger Pinckney	Dwayne Wells
Donald C. Butts	Colin Greenwood	Kevin McCormack	Charlie Price	Arthur W. Wheaton
Timothy Carney	Daryl D. Hallquist	Chris McGann	Michael Sabbeth	Donald Whittaker
Paul E. Chase	Bill Hammond	Michael McIntosh	Carlos Schmidt	G.H. Whittome
John Curnow	Nick Hahn	Colin McLagan	Ned Schwing	Stuart M. Williams
Donald Dallas	Jonathan Hanson	Lt. Col. Ridgely Marriott, III	Charles Semmer	R.L. Wilson
Bill Davis	Eldridge Hardie	Don Masters	Ross Seyfried	Bill Wise

Daniel Philip Côté	Joanna Lynn Côté	Heidi Haven	Glen Horton
Editor/Publisher/ArtDirector	Editor	Fulfilment	Assistant Editor

THE DOUBLE GUN JOURNAL (ISSN 1050-2262) is published quarterly by *The Double Gun Journal*, Incorporated—P.O. Box 550, East Jordan, Michigan 49727 ©2003 by *The Double Gun Journal*. All rights reserved. **Periodical Postage** is paid at East Jordan, Michigan and additional offices. **Subscription Rate** $39.95 for one year, Canada and Mexico add $10/surface, $24/ air per year, U. S. Funds. Outside North America add $12/surface, P.O.R./air, U. S. Funds. Address all **subscription correspondence and advertising queries** to *The Double Gun Journal*, P.O.Box 550, East Jordan, Michigan 49727. All manuscripts, letters, photography and artwork delivered to *The Double Gun Journal* are considered our property—with all publishing rights—unless otherwise stated in writing with original submission. A self-addressed postage paid container of proper size must be included for the return of all submissions. We cannot guarantee against damage to or loss of materials submitted. Address all editorial, advertising and other correspondence to *The Double Gun Journal*, P.O. Box 550, East Jordan, Michigan 49727. Telephone: 231-536-7439. Fax: 231-536-7450 Send or fax **address changes** to *The Double Gun Journal*, Subscriptions Department, P.O. Box 550, East Jordan, Michigan 49727.
COPYRIGHT 2003 BY *THE DOUBLE GUN JOURNAL, INC.* ALL RIGHTS RESERVED.
POSTMASTER: Please send address changes and inquiries to *The Double Gun Journal*, P.O. Box 550, East Jordan, Michigan 49727 U.S.A.

The Double Gun Journal

VOLUME FOURTEEN   ISSUE 3   2003

To a good many of us there is no thrill in the sporting line to compare with the hunting of grouse and woodcock. I use the word 'hunting' with premeditation, for 'shooting' is a poor term and does not fit the case. We hunt, and we hunt on foot, many miles for every grouse bagged, and this is not forgetting the hunting we do by car, exploring back roads of inconceivable awfulness, map in hand. The more disreputable the road, the better chance we have of finding undisturbed bird covers. As we wallow along on these little exploration trips, our eyes are fastened to the landscape at imminent risk of lodging the car in some bottomless gutter. We may go for days on a pocket full of shells. Shooting is only incidental, but the lure of pioneering is always with us.

I have often tried to explain the fascination of New England grouse hunting to those who have shot only quail and ducks, or perhaps Scotch grouse and English partridge. But this is a waste of time, for such folk cannot understand the expenditure of time, energy, and gasoline for a bag which, measured in meat, is scarcely worth a fraction of the effort we put into it. No, a 'dyed-in-the-wool' grouse hunter is just a plain crank. For my part, I'm heartily glad there are no more of them, for then surely poor old *Bonasa* would be in a sad way.

I sometimes wonder what the future has in store for the youngsters who are coming along—the human youngsters I mean. Will there be any chance for them to enjoy even a taste of the thrills we have had? Is there anything that we can do to delay what looks like an inevitable day of reckoning?

Excerpted from The Future of Grouse Hunting In New England, A Sportsman's Second Scrapbook, *by John C. Phillips. Courtesy of the Houghton Mifflin Company, 1933.*

William Harnden Foster

Crossing Shot - Grouse
Watercolour
Painted by Eldridge Hardie

VACHERON CONSTANTIN
Manufacture Horlogère Genève.

Malte Dual Time Regulator

From time's finest Craftsmen

Since 1755.

‖‖‖ MANFREDI

121 Greenwich Ave   Greenwich CT 06830
(203) 622-1414   (866) 843-7655   Fax: (203) 622-1567
www.manfredijewels.com   info@manfredijewels.com

Having Your Cake And Eating It

It's time to rethink your mutual fun. Think of your Merkel as a sound investment both monetarily and mentally. Merkel rifles and combination guns can actually gain in value while you use them, and have historically done so. We offer a wide range of options — from Safari and double rifles to drillings and the all-new K-1 lightweight single-shot stalking rifle. And there are no brokerage fees. So go ahead, have your cake and eat it. Visit your Merkel dealer today for the investment of a lifetime that lasts a lifetime. For a full-color catalog visit our web site at www.gsifirearms.com or send a written request to the address below.

The Blue-Winged Teal Of Chone

*Written and Photographed
by Nick Hahn*

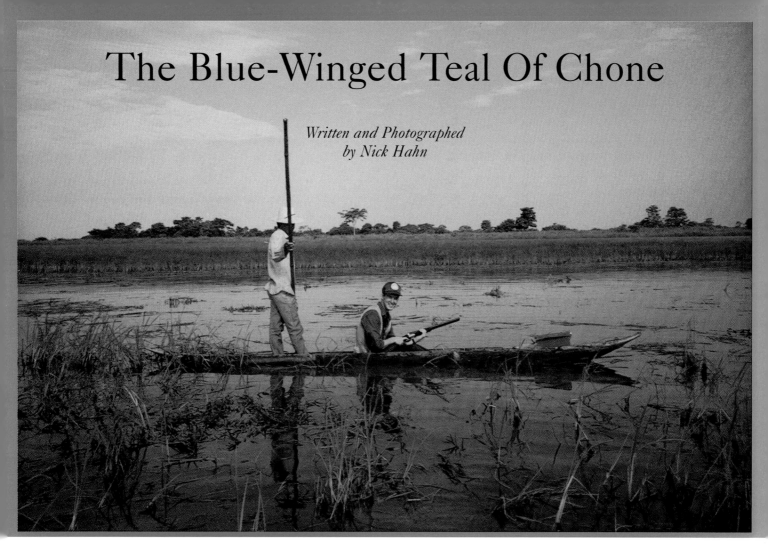

Chone is located at the northern end of Manabi province, in Ecuador, about five hours' ride from Guayaquil. The amazing thing about Chone is that it is located in an ecosystem that has its own microclimate. As you drive through typical Manabi terrain, you find yourself suddenly in a bowl, surrounded by low hills that are green. The bottom of the bowl is crisscrossed with streams and rivulets, all ending in a large, expansive, shallow lake. It is completely unlike the rest of Manabi, indeed, the rest of Ecuador for that matter. Each year, starting in about mid-October, blue-winged teal from North America find their way to Chone. Some of the birds fly down all the way from Canada! The teal congregate in Chone in fantastic numbers, and each year a handful of duck hunters from Guayaquil and Quito, the two major population centers in Ecuador, used to journey to that region to sample some incredible duck shooting. During my two tours in Ecuador, the annual trip to Chone became a tradition. I used to contact my friends at the United States Embassy in Quito, located in the higher altitude, six hours' drive from Guayaquil, and we would arrange to meet in Chone. Usually at least a half a dozen duck hunters would come down from Quito, while from Guayaquil, it was my friend Lorenzo and I, and Bill Fitzgerald, the only other shooter from the U.S. Consulate General in Guayaquil. We would meet in Chone, set up a camp near the water. There were no

hotels nearby, and the town of Chone was a bit too far from the duck-shooting area, so we had to sleep in tents. Usually this created a somewhat festive atmosphere, as everyone pitched tents and set up their "camp." We brought our own food, since it would have been impractical to drive into town to eat, then have to come back and set up camp. We couldn't very well leave our camp unattended. Lorenzo was always the one tasked with finding "retrievers," young boys willing to fetch ducks for pay. After the boys were found and told to come to our campsite before light, we would tend to the camp. Sometimes, if it was still early, some of the guys would go dove shooting in the surrounding hills. But most of the time we simply got ready for the morning. All the scouting was done before camp was made.

In the morning the various groups would split up, taking their "retrievers" with them, heading out to pre-designated hot spots. Most of the spots were reachable on foot, but sometimes we had to hire canoes to get to the more isolated regions. We always tried to spread out, since the area was very large and there just weren't enough hunters or enough pressure on the birds to keep them moving. Sometimes if our groups were too small, we hired a local fisherman who had an outboard motor to circle the lake and keep the birds moving. For these birds from the north, decoys worked well. The shooting was always good. Some years it was better than others, but overall, always good. As in other locations

Bill Fitzgerald getting out to his blind with the help of a local dug-out canoe.

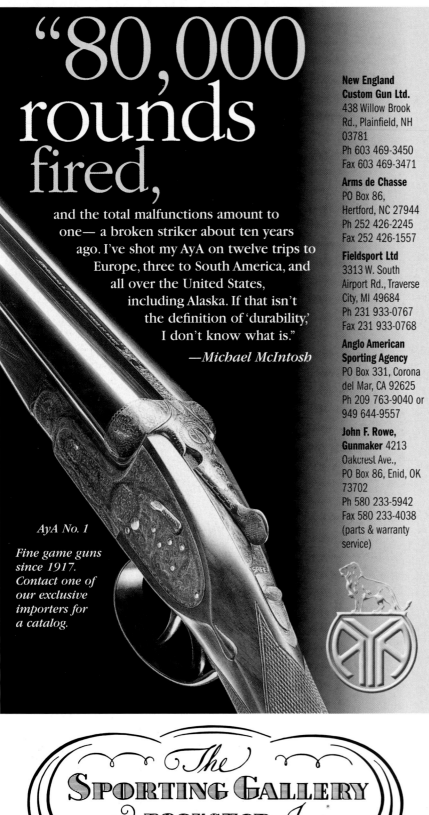

in Ecuador, we did not use chest waders or hip boots. The weather was simply too warm, so we got wet, usually standing knee deep in water while shooting.

The blue-winged teal is a small bird, about the size of a pigeon. As long as you don't try to shoot them at nosebleed altitudes, normal trap loads will suffice. I used exactly the same loads on blue wings as I did on Santa Cruz pigeons, No. 7$\frac{1}{2}$ trap loads, and never experienced any problems. My friend Lorenzo, on the other hand, insisted on using heavy "duck" loads. I could never figure out why Lorenzo always used these "teeth rattling" heavy loads. He is a superb wing shot, and normal loads would have been more than adequate in his hands. But, he insisted on heavy loads, and sometimes after extensive shooting, he would develop a headache from recoil! All his guns took a beating. Lorenzo shot a custom-ordered Bernardelli double (especially made to handle heavy loads) and an old but heavy proof W.W. Greener with 30-inch barrels. I shot 12-bore doubles, over and unders and side by sides. For some reason which now escapes me, I mostly shot over and unders, Perazzi and Merkel. My friends from our embassy in Quito used to arrive with an assortment of weaponry. One fellow showed up one year with an old hammer gun. He didn't do so well, so the following year he brought a modern over and under. Another fellow, from the Defense Attache's Office, was armed with an 18-inch barreled military shotgun with a folding stock. I don't believe he got a single bird, despite the fact that the teal literally dive-bombed his blind.

Shooting blue-winged teal in Chone, Ecuador, is a unique experience. Some of the birds we shot were banded, and most of the banded birds were from the United States pothole country. However, there were a few that were banded in Canada. The people in Chone say that the teal make the sound of a motor as they fly by in their typical manner. Indeed, the wings do make a peculiar rushing sound. But I am not too sure it sounds like a motor.

Editor's Note: The author lived and worked on five continents as a United States Foreign Service Officer. His last two postings were as U.S. Consul General to Egypt and to Mexico respectively. He is currently retired in Arizona with his wife, Jo, and a neurotic German wirehaired pointer named Logan.

British Doubles From A to Z

Part XVII

Written and Photographed
by Sherman Bell

We continue our study of the Birmingham gunmaker, W. & C. Scott. One purpose of the *A to Z* series, beyond treating our eyes to the beauty and quality of British doubles, is to study the evolution of British gunmaking, including those variations that had only limited success. By progressing from oldest to newest through a large number of guns from one maker, we will see how the designs advanced and how the changing demand from buyers shaped the company's products.

We now look at gun No. 2829, made in 1871. As we study this gun we immediately notice an inconsistency in the serial number and date of production from earlier Scott guns that were made in 1866 but had serial numbers above 11000. The answer to this mystery is that there were two parallel series of serial numbers for guns produced from 1865 through 1878. One series started with No. 1 in 1865 and ended in 1878 with a serial number under 11000. The other series started at No. 11000 in 1866 and reached No. 23999 by 1878. From 1878 onward there is just one series that continued in ascending order, from number 24000 through the end of production. But during the overlap period from 1866 through 1878, a later gun may have a lower

serial number and vice versa. The only way to make sense of it is to refer to the Scott book to see which year each block of serial numbers was assigned to. Thus we find that No. 2829 was made five years later than gun No. 11957, which we looked at in the last *A to Z* article.

W. & C. Scott No. 2829 is the first of several Premier Grade guns that grace this series. The dictionary definition of the word *Premier* includes the following: "of the first rank, first in position, rank or importance, outstanding." Premier-Grade Scott guns are the most expensive and most highly finished models that Scott produced. There were even special ranks among Premier guns, as we shall see later, but the Premier designation is associated with only the best guns. This veteran 10-gauge gun reminds me of an elderly lady, whose best days are far behind her but who still has the breeding and grace of an aristocrat. She is aged and worn from the trials of the years and has suffered a few indignities; indeed, the signs that she was once a beauty are hard to find. But by her name and title you know the glory of her youth.

This 10-pound gun with 30-inch Damascus barrels has likely seen the migration of more wildfowl than any of us can dream of today. Judging from the signs of extensive

W. & C. Scott guns in serial numbers 2999 and 2829 (bottom).

use, it has participated in the harvest of many of those birds. The bores are actually in quite good shape. Measuring the barrels we find that although originally marked at 11 gauge, they now both measure .779 inch. The maximum measurement for an 11-gauge gun is .762 inch, so a clean-up bore and polish of at least .017 inch has taken place,

top lever has a mushy feeling when closing. This is a sure sign that a blacksmith has been at work and indeed we see signs of welded metal on the barrel hook. It is true that building up the hook surface can be done correctly to put a gun back on face, but this gun was repaired improperly. The irony is, it was totally unnecessary to touch the hook surface because this gun has Scott's patent adjustable lump feature, patented by William M. Scott under British patent No. 452 in 1870. The Scott book tells us that this patent feature was used on better quality hammer guns from 1870 to 1887. This adjustable feature has a moveable center section in the hook area of the front lump. By removing a small lock screw on the bottom of the lump, the larger adjustment pin may be advanced part of a turn. This adjustment screw advances a wedge, to move the hook surface forward and take up the wear-gap between the pin and lump.

On this and facing page: W. & C. Scott serial number 2999.

This 10-gauge hammer gun balances about 1/2 inch in front of the hinge pin. The straight-grip stock has a pull of 14-1/4 inches and a drop of 1-3/4 inches x 3 inches. As with all Premier Grade Scott guns it is fully and finely engraved. Unfortunately the gun hackers have been at it and the engraving is pretty well destroyed by buffing and then re-case coloring over the buffed metal. This is like putting a new shiny paint job on a wrecked car without doing the proper bodywork first—it just doesn't look right. This haphazard gun-butchery is the bane of old firearms. I wish the amateur "restorers," would take up working on farm implements or diesel trucks and leave fine firearms to the few talented workman who do it right. The "restoration" market is driven by those who seek old guns and then want them to look new. There is nothing wrong with honest wear on a fine weapon. Signs of use are mute testimony of adventures lived long ago and hunting successes, now shrouded by the veil of time.

So in spite of my merciless critique, we must reflect on all the fun that the previous owners have had in the process of putting this gun in its present worn state. The 132-year history of this gun includes an era when the skies turned dark with passing fowl. It is pretty clear to me that this old 10-gauge gun was in the thick of it.

explaining why the bores look better than the balance of the gun. The old barrels still ring true and have cylinder boring, both sides. The rib inscription reads "W. & C. Scott & Son [The Premier Quality] 10 Gt. Castle St. Regent Circus, London." The barrels of this well-used gun are off the face as evidenced by the gap between the breech face and the barrels. The barrels do not wiggle however and the

The next Scott gun is a very nice medium-grade hammer gun, serial number 2999, also made in 1871. This is a 10-gauge rebounding hammer bar-action gun with the Scott spindle and top-lever opening system. It has 31-1/2 inch

Damascus barrels, a straight-grip stock of figured walnut with 14-5/16 inch pull length to a horn plate, 1-3/4 inch x 2-1/2 inch drop and a forend with a cross-wedge retainer. The point of balance is 3/4 inch ahead of the cross pin. The weight is 8-1/4 pounds which is about what a 12-bore pigeon or waterfowl gun weighs. No, all 10-bore guns are not heavy, ungainly magnums. This is a prime example of the wonderful 10s chambered for non-magnum shorter shells; this one has 2-5/8 inch chambers.

A closer look at the barrels shows an inscription on the

not make the common mistake of writing off these early cylinder-bored guns as useless relics. The effectiveness of a good-quality gun with glass-smooth barrels that have straight boring was brought home to me again, just recently. A few of us double gun fanatics have set up our own sporting-clays course centered around a retired dairy barn on a rural farm property. We can shoot here any time we like and another benefit over a fixed course is our ability to shoot a station from any angle or distance we want. The last time out I found myself a full 40 yards from the point at

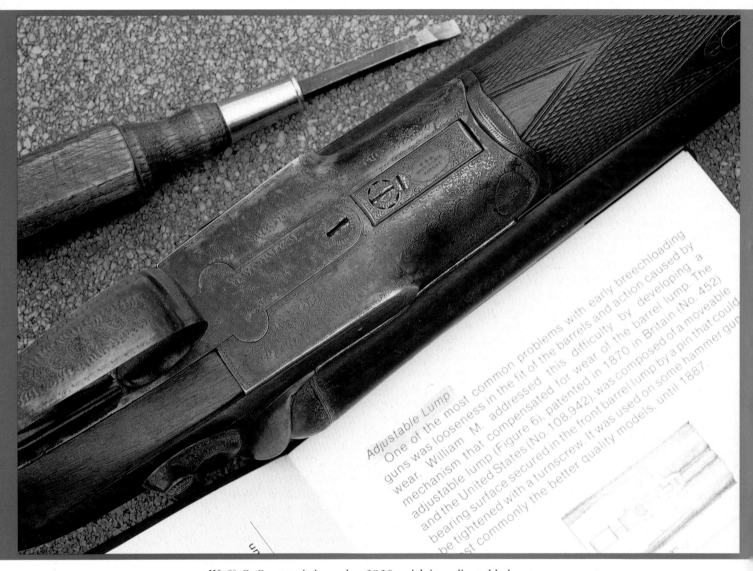

Adjustable Lump
One of the most common problems with early breechloading guns was looseness in the fit of the barrels and action caused by wear. William M. addressed this difficulty by developing a mechanism that compensated for wear of the barrel lump. The adjustable lump (Figure 6), patented in 1870 in Britain (No. 452) and the United States (No. 108,942), was composed of a moveable bearing surface secured in the front barrel lump by a pin that could be tightened with a turnscrew. It was used on some hammer gun most commonly the better quality models, until 1887.

W. & C. Scott serial number 2829, with its adjustable lump.

smooth concave top rib that reads: "W. & C. Scott & Son, Patentees, 10 Gt. Castle St. Regent Circus, London". Starting in 1872, one year after this medium-grade gun was made, the address of the showroom at 10 Great Castle Street, London, was used only on "A" and "B" Grade Scott guns. This practice continued through 1897, when Webley & Scott was formed. Flipping the barrels over, we find only the basic London proofs that were required under the rules of 1868. Both barrels now measure .782 inch, which is well in proof for the "10" marks on the flats. Before the rule changes of 1875 there were no marks to designate choke boring.

This early gun does not have choke in either barrel. Do

which the fast clays exited the barn window and they didn't get any closer as they flew. I found that with the cylinder-bored right barrel of a 12-gauge Boswell I could break the clay when I managed to haul the barrels way out in front and keep them moving. Did I mention that this was with a load of only 7/8 ounce of No. 7-1/2 shot? Oh yes, I should also mention that the clays were the little 60mm size, not the big pie-plate 108s. Now don't get me wrong, a cylinder bored gun is not a reliable clean-killer of game at 40 yards—especially tough birds like waterfowl or pheasant. But when a pheasant flushes at 25 yards from the muzzles of a good cylinder gun, don't bet the lunch money he will get away. Useless cylinder bore? Not hardly!

The larger bore of a ten-gauge gun can only improve the performance of any given charge of shot fired from a twelve. Arm yourself with a fine ten bore such as this one and 1-1/4 ounce loads of lead 5s and head for pheasant cover with confidence. From first-hand experience, I can tell you, that Scott gun No. 2999, and others of its kind, would not let you down.

In 1872, W. & C. Scott made gun No. 16886. This gun is numbered in the parallel series that began with No. 11000 in 1866. This 12-gauge hammer gun is another medium grade piece that does not have any outstanding features but is a good solid gun. The locks are the back-action non-rebounding type. The action has ~~a sidelever on the starboard side that~~ engages a sliding underbolt. Unlike many later guns, there is only a single bite in the rear barrel lug. To some, sidelever guns might appear to be awkward to manipulate, but in actual use they are quite handy. Guns with a right-hand sidelever, like this one, are quite easy to use. Going further, the left-hand sidelever guns are an absolute dream for a right-handed shooter, requiring less grip-shift to open them than either the top or right-hand sidelever guns. As with most aspects of the gun world, a day's field experience actually using a gun beats a month of reading the armchair expert's opinions about it.

The subject of armchair experts reminds me of a recent occasion; I was socializing after hours with some folks I had just met at a big antique arms show. Naturally the talk centered on guns and shooting. One fellow recognized my byline and after some conversation asked a question. Did I actually shoot those old guns featured in my articles—even the ones with Damascus barrels—or did I just write about them? I nearly spilled my refreshment and I am sure my mouth became a good fly-trap! I must be naïve; I cannot imagine writing about something I had not actually done or experienced first-hand. Please be assured that I actually do shoot them and the *Double Gun Journal* is the place to come for real-world information.

Now back to gun No. 16886. This 6-3/4 pound hammer gun has 28-inch laminated steel barrels. Pape's patent on choke-boring would not lapse for another year when this gun was made; like most guns of this era it has no choke. Bores measure .725 inch and .722 inch right and left which is slightly oversized for the 13-gauge proof marks stamped in the underside of the

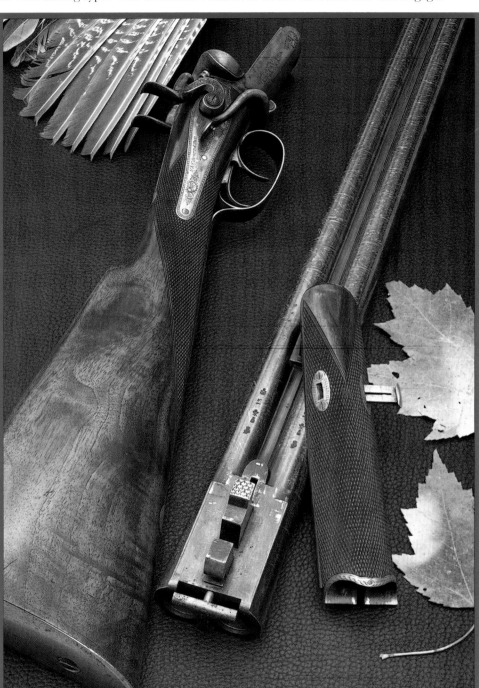

On this and facing page: W. & C. Scott serial number 16886.

barrels; the range for 13 gauge being .710 inch to .718 inch. The stock is of classic straight-grip style of decent walnut. The dimensions are straight but the length of pull is quite short at only 13-1/2 inches. This would be a great gun for a youngster or a lady of smaller stature. It is light in weight, it's British and it has Damascus barrels—what's not to love?

We move a year ahead to 1875 and Scott 12-gauge gun No. 6531. This gun embodies several patent features designed by W.M. Scott. The oldest is the spindle with top snap patented in 1865. This is paired with the double under-bolt patented by James Purdey in 1863. The forend latch on this gun is the push-in type patented by Scott in 1873. But the most

noticeable feature, is the unusual—almost bizarre—"Scott's Patent Quadruple Bolt" locking system. In addition to the twin underbolts there is also another pair of locking bolts. On the outer edge of the standing breech we find bolts that work parallel to the barrels and lock in mating projections of each side of the barrel breech face. Can you imagine trying to joint this mechanical nightmare so that all four sets of bites and bolts function properly? One questions if the extra bolts performed a necessary function and this must have also occurred to gun buyers of the day; it was not a big seller. We are fortunate to have two examples of this very unusual patented gun to study, because only a few guns of this type were made during the 1870s and the Scott patent 2052 of 1874 was allowed to die quietly.

W. & C. Scott serial number 6531 with unique "quad-lock."

This rare Scott quad-lock is a bar-action gun with rebounding-hammers and odd-length 29-5/8 inch Damascus barrels. The barrel flats carry the basic London proofs and gauge marks for 13 bore. These barrels have undergone a clean-up bore to improve their condition, as they now measure .733 inch and .734 inch right and left. In addition is the legend "Charge 3 Drms. 1-1/8 Shot." Although this gun is made during 1875, it must have passed through the proof house before the new rules of that year took effect. It has strong modified boring in both tubes but there are no "not for ball" marks used to designate choke boring during the period from 1875 through 1887.

On this and facing page: W. & C. Scott, serial number 6531 utilizes the "Scott's Patent Quadruple Bolt" locking system.

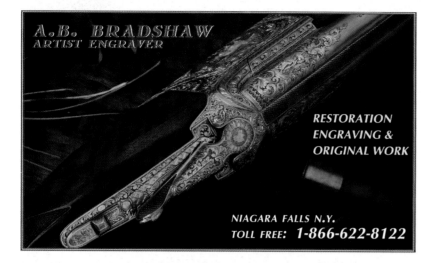
The round-knob pistol-grip stock is of good quality well-figured wood. This fancy figure carries into the grip area and may be responsible for the crack that runs from the right side of the action upper tang, on through the right-side lockplate area and terminates underneath at the trigger plate. Fancy wood grain is wonderful to look at, but grain-flow in the head and grip area of a stock should be straight for best strength. The stock dimensions are unusable for me with a 2-inch drop at comb and 3 inch at heel. The length is 14 inches. The fellow who ordered this gun must have been a stout lad with a very full face. This is a high-grade gun with much, fine scroll engraving on the action. The rib carries the 10 Great Castle Street address, indicative of "A" and "B" quality guns. This 7³/₄ pound gun balances a half inch ahead of the hinge pin. It has a good feel to it and if not for the droopy stock dimensions I would be happy to let the fine Damascus

*W. & C. Scott
serial number 5748, 10-gauge.*

barrels with modified chokes help me harvest a few duck dinners.

Scott gun No. 5748 was made in 1874. As mentioned in the *A to Z* part 16 article, about half of the hammer guns made by Scott from 1865 through 1880 were based on various types of actions with features patented by other makers. Premier-grade gun No. 5748 is one of these, a 10-gauge hammer gun that has a thumb-snap action, patented by James Purdey. The Scott book states that *most* of the non-Scott action guns were made as B & C Grade guns and numbered in the 11000 to 23000 range. This gun runs counter to that, by being a Premier-Grade best-quality piece and having a serial number in the lower range, below 11000. In the study of old British firearms the words "always" and "never" are for fools, or those who wish to soon be made the fool, when another unusual specimen shows up.

This robust 10-gauge gun has 30-inch Damascus barrels and a pistol-grip stock. The stock has a gold three-point shield inlaid in the grip, just aft of the top tang. This is the signature feature of a Premiere Grade gun. The weight is 10-1/4 pounds that balances 1/2 inch ahead

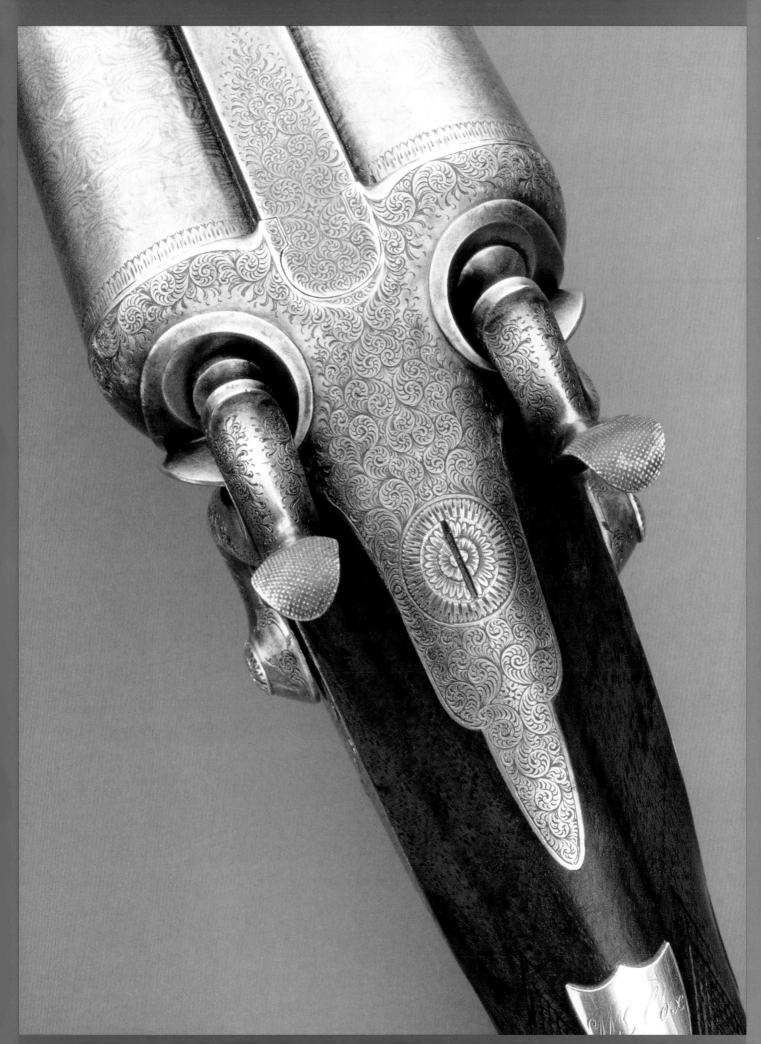

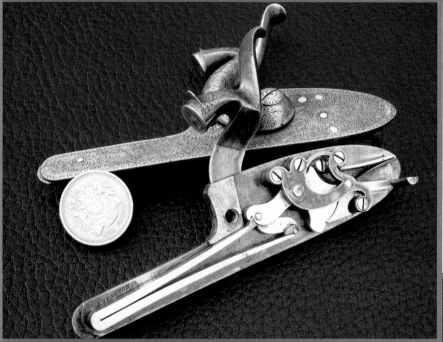

W & C. SCOTT & SON [The Premier Quality] 10. G⁴ CAST

On this and facing page: W. & C. Scott serial number 5748, Purdey thumb snap-action and best-quality J. Stanton locks.

of the hinge pin. Being made before the proof rules of 1875 there are no choke markings on the barrel flats. However, the legend "Charge 4 drams 1 1/4 Shot" engraved on the right barrel flat tells us the intended load and a most deadly one it is. In addition, the legend "The Premier Gun", is on the left barrel flat. Most likely, this early gun originally had cylinder bores. It now has jug chokes of about improved cylinder and modified constriction. My collector face frowns at this rude

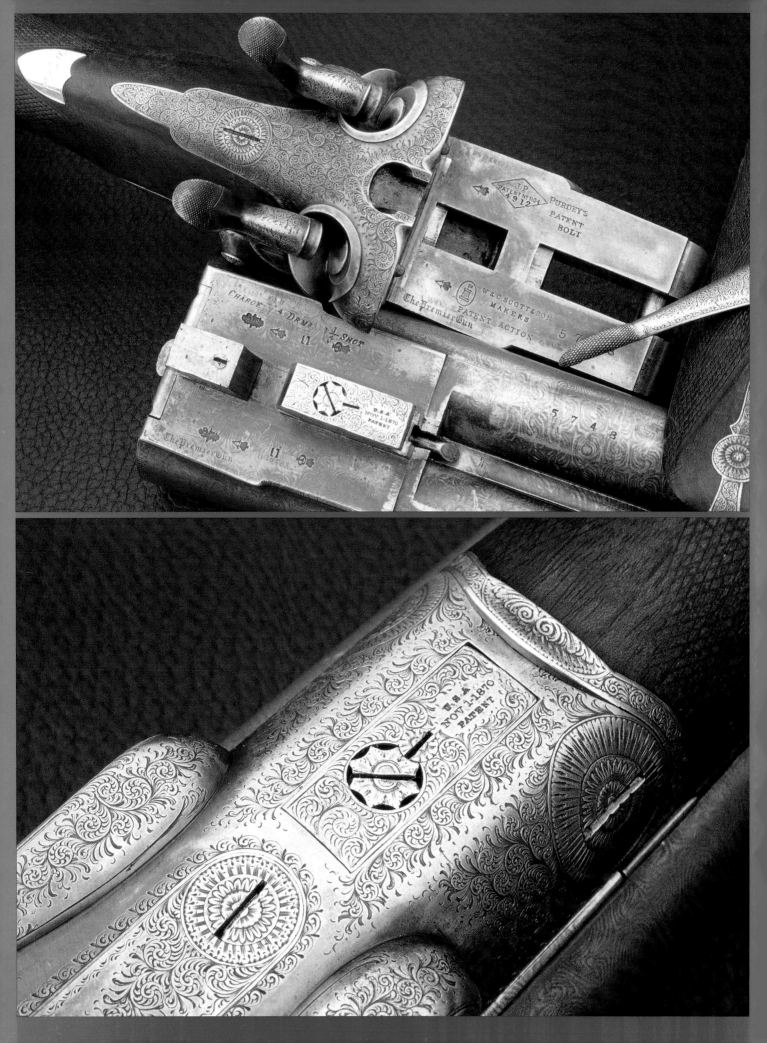

violation and as we discussed earlier, a cylinder bore is still quite effective. However, I must admit jug-choking does work to tighten pattern performance, if done correctly. If it gets an excellent old British 10-gauge gun like this one out of the closet and into the game fields or duck flats, then perhaps I can overlook the indiscretion.

The thumb lever, accessed through the open front of the triggerguard, moves a typical Purdey double-sliding underbolt. The bar-action locks are rebounding and the flat-faced hammers and large-faced firing pins show very little wear. Original case color is strong on the action body. The action filer, the finisher, and the engraver who worked on this gun were masters of their craft. In this undamaged Premier-Grade gun, we finally get to see what best-grade Scott workmanship is all about. The surfaces of the action and furniture have coverage of fine engraving, in this case tight scrollwork. The forend lever and finial also have fine engraving and the lever tip has very fine checkering. The hammer spurs and the underside of the thumb lever have even finer checkering of stunning quality. Deeply chiseled percussion fences and the complex form of the action bars show us, once again, what extraordinary skill and pride in workmanship existed in the British gun trade of the 19th century. This workmanship goes much deeper than the outside appearance. I am a bit of a lock freak. I pulled the plates from this old 10 bore and treated my eyes to the sight of pristine best-quality locks signed by J. Stanton. The bridles are four-pin, of superlative quality with all the case colors intact. These locks are also a treat to the ears and to the touch as they snick and click in precise movement.

This lovely Premier gun also has the adjustable lump feature we encountered before and with this gun we had the opportunity to see how this feature works when it is untampered with. This original-condition Scott gun had a fair degree of looseness in the fit of barrels to breech, as I received it. I applied

W. & C. Scott serial number 5748, showing the Purdey double sliding underbolt and barrel lump adjustment screw.

penetrating oil around the adjustment mechanism and waited days for it to invade this moveable mechanism that had not moved for 129 years. I then cautiously advanced the lump adjustment screw 1.8 of a turn. This removed all looseness and the gun is now tight as new and will require some shooting to bring the lockup from tight to normal. Who knows, in another 100 years or so it may require another 1/8 turn! For now, all this fine gun needs is some 10-gauge, 2-7/8 inch shells, holding 1-1/4 ounce of Bismuth shot and a steady guiding hand to push its barrels in front of some passing mallards. I am very sure it remembers how to do the rest.

We close this entry in our continuing look at the guns from W. & C. Scott with an old soldier that has earned retirement—but did not go quietly into that great good night. Scott gun number 20601 was made in 1875. This is a bar-action 10-gauge hammer gun with rebounding locks. This wide-breeched old gun weighs 10-1/2 pounds. It has an unusual opening system, but other than that it is about as plain-finished and unremarkable as you are likely to see in a British-made double gun. There is no engraving and the top rib inscription reads simply, "W. & C. Scott & Son Makers, London."

The most remarkable feature of this gun comes not from its makers but from its owners. It is remarkable how much it has been used! It is not merely worn, it is just about completely worn out! The owner or owners past, did not give up on the old gun easily. It must have had shooting qualities considered very valuable to someone. After recoil from untold thousands of rounds, the stock split through the grip and head area. Someone made a repair with glue and tightly wound copper wire, complete with wood screws to retain the wire ends—and the gun kept on shooting. I must admire the tenacity and ingenuity of this home-repair nimrod, if not his advanced gunsmithing skills. This repair is, itself, ancient. The copper coils binding the stock wrist have worn smooth and take on a utilitarian charm that matches the balance of this thoroughly used double gun. The stock

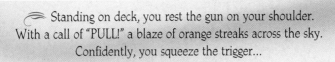

has re-split from years of post-repair shooting, but the old wire repair held—and the gun kept on shooting. We must assume that this plain-grade gun was owned by a succession of working-class hunters to whom the value of a gun was a substantial investment. Wear and stock cracks were no reason to give up on a valued hunting companion; the important thing was to keep the old gun working. It must have worked for untold thousands of rounds.

The heavy Damascus barrels are much brighter on the outside than on the inside. As might be expected, the bores are rough and pitted but they are proofed at 11 gauge and still measure in-spec at .759 inch and .757 inch! The length is an odd 29 inches and at the present muzzles we find the beginnings of choke constrictions; they have been lopped off. Well what the heck—it still shot alright after the damaged muzzles, complete with chokes, went under the hacksaw—and it kept on shooting. At some time the loop parted ways with the barrels and was re-soldered crudely back in place. It kept on shooting. At another time in the gun's long history, one of the hammers was broken and a crude-looking replacement was swapped in. And it kept on shooting.

After all this, the old Damascus tubes ring true and could still be shot if the balance of the gun would hold together around them. Those who expound about how fragile Damascus barrels are and how any rust and pitting renders them unsafe, would do well to study this set of plain-grade barrels. They have survived the nineteenth and twentieth centuries, the firing of a large truckload of black powder shells and I would guess quite a few cases of full nitro loads and are still basically sound today. But perhaps this actual physical evidence would be too confusing to an expert.

The barrel-locking mechanism of this old warrior is a bit unusual. The opening lever, located inside an elongated and rather ugly triggerguard, looks for all the world like a backward-mounted third trigger. Pushing this lever forward causes a sliding bolt to retract into the breech and release the barrels. This bolt locks into a single bite cut into the rear barrel lump. The bite slot is cut on an upward angle to give a light cam action to close the gun.

"W. & C. Scott & Son Makers, London" serial number 20601. This gun was made in 1875.

An upward extension of the locking bolt also has an angled surface. A projection on the rear barrel lump contacts this ramp and forces the sliding bolt to the rear as the gun is closed and then allows it to snap into lockup as the barrels come tight to the breech. The mechanism is similar to several others patented in the 1860s such as Horsley's and Agnew's. Both used a lever mounted in front of the triggers to activate a sliding single-bolt locking mechanism.

The bottom of the front barrel lump on this gun has "D.N. Sherman's Patent" prominently engraved thereon. I have not found reference to this patent, even in Crudgington & Baker's wonderful two volume set, *The British Shotgun*. In any event this patent is not materially different from numerous others of the period. However this gun, made in 1875, is a rather late application of a design that had its day and was already superseded by newer schemes. Like the sidelever guns, this action is quick and easy to open.

"W. & C. Scott & Son
Makers, London"

This gun balances 1-1/4 inch in front of the hinge pin. The drop is a low 1-7/8 inches x 3-1/4 inches with a pull length of 14-1/2 inches. The drop dimensions are totally unusable for me, but they must have suited someone just fine for it has been used and used and used! How I would love to know the sum of its bag, the events witnessed and the masters served. The present owner who contributed several Scott guns to this series, commented that I might not want to include this worn gun. But in fact, Scott No. 20601 is an interesting example of extensive faithful service provided by a plain but properly made British double. It is a history book with the past written upon its worn surface. I only wish we could de-code the story in detail. No, I did not exclude this honest old gun because of its worn condition and it is my hope that a "restorer" never comes within a mile of it!

When our trip through the collection of guns from W. & C. Scott continues, we will begin to visit the glorious 1880s, when British gunmaking was in full bloom and approaching the zenith of its glory.

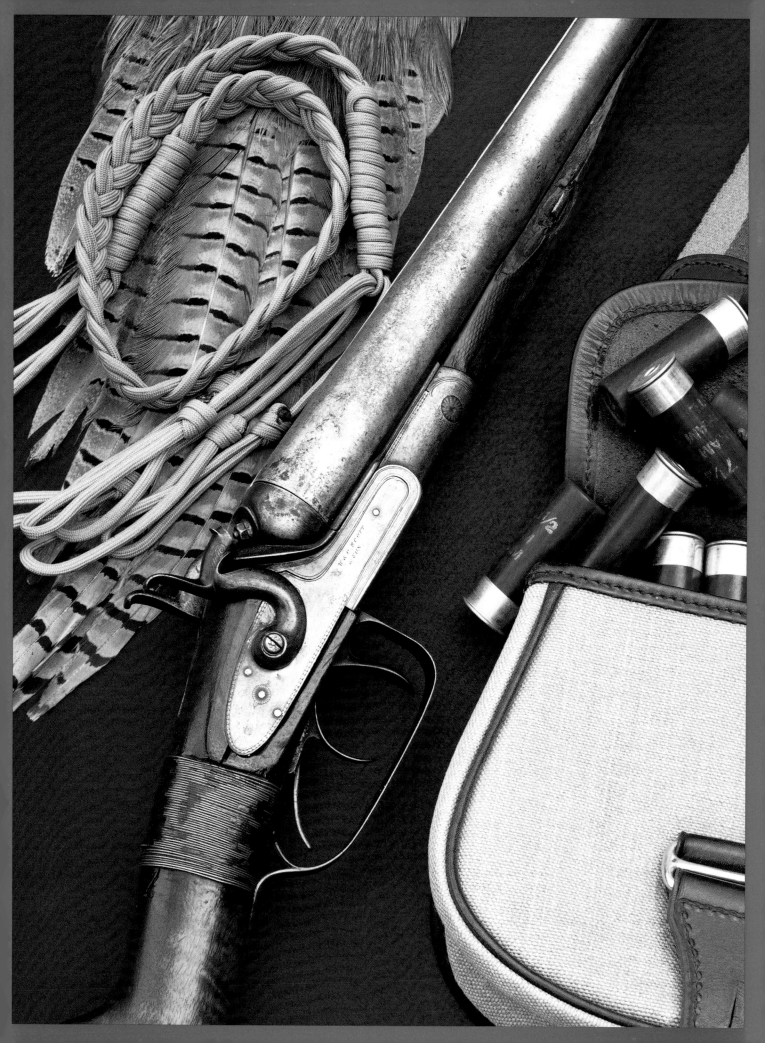

BRAYS ISLAND... THE STANDARD FOR OUTDOOR SPORTING COMMUNITIES

For lovers of sport – and connoisseurs of the good life – there is no place quite like Brays Island Plantation.

Sporting Classics magazine hailed this private sporting community as "the South's most outstanding residential sporting community – the one by which all others are judged." The Orvis Company awarded its first U.S. endorsement of a private facility to Brays Island, recognizing its world-class hunting – complete with experienced guides, trained bird dogs, private stocks of quail and cut grain fields for exciting dove shoots. Indeed, life at this plantation, located near the South Carolina coast between Charleston and Savannah, is defined by close interaction with nature and appreciation for sport and outdoor pursuits.

Since 3,500 of the island's 5,500 acres remain untouched in vast nature preserves, the unique lifestyle, world-class sporting amenities and well-designed homes at Brays Island are reserved for a select few who enjoy the best of life and the great outdoors. Surrounded by 20 miles of waterways, Brays Island's unsurpassed location puts its 325 owners just minutes from first-class saltwater fishing for redfish, tarpon, sea trout and more. The private 18-hole golf course incorporates elements of traditional Scottish links courses with no tee-time required, while the plantation's elegant main house, now restored as the Inn at Brays Island, offers riverfront dining and accommodations for owners and their guests. A well-appointed Gun Club and Equestrian Center, full-service marina, plus an Owners' Services staff to help make the most of it all prove that there is no other private community quite like Brays Island.

Call **843-846-3100** or toll free **866-320-1201** today for more information and to arrange a personal visit. Homesites from under $150,000 to $750,000. Homes from $675,000 to 2.7 million.

Brays Island
R E A L T Y , L L C

115 Brays Island Drive • Sheldon, South Carolina 29941
866.320.1201 • 843.846.3100 • www.huntbraysisland.com

Bonhams 1793
& BUTTERFIELDS
AUCTIONEERS & APPRAISERS

Modern Sporting Guns
Tuesday December 9, 10am

Inquiries
Paul Carella (415) 503 3360
Paul.Carella@bonhams.com

Roger Lake (415) 503 3445
Roger.Lake@bonhams.com

We are now accepting consignments for our December auction. This sale features over 150 American, British and European shotguns and rifles. Makers include: Parker, Remington, L.C. Smith, Fox, Winchester, Browning and James Purdey & Sons.

Call for complimentary auction estimates.

Pictured:
Rare Parker BHE 12 Ga. D.B. Shotgun with 34 in. barrels.
Estimate: $6,000 - 8,000

Parker VHE .410 D.B. Shotgun.
Estimate: $5,000 - 7,000

The Syracuse Arms Co.

Part III

Model Variation

by Tom Archer
Photography by Terry Allen

History records the years from 1890 through 1910 as a period of rapid change in the United States; a period of innovation, modification, and progressive improvement in the objects, matters, and mechanical devices intended to create a more profitable, rewarding, and comfortable human existence. Constant change and consumer demand promoted intense competition among the various makers and suppliers of goods and services, which resulted in entirely new industries and products while, at the same time, relegating others to obsolescence.

The American shotgun is illustrative of the changes that occurred during this era. The invention of more powerful smokeless powders dictated development of stronger gun frames and bolting designs. These new powders increased barrel pressures necessitating new gun-barrel steels, as the integrity of even the finest Damascus barrels came under suspicion. Additionally, American double-gun makers of the period saw the introduction and rapid acceptance of very efficient, reliable, and less costly repeating shotguns. To the twenty-first century student of the American double gun, competitive pressures on gun design and production are evident in all period maker's products by visual comparison of early to later serial-numbered guns in surviving examples. Ultimately, economic and competitive pressures combined with a soft demand to topple even the most prestigious American double-gun makers, but the resultant attempts of their respective efforts to compete greatly enhanced the study and collecting of the guns themselves. With the possible exception of the Baker, the best-known American double-gun makers have received, to varying degrees, considerable press detailing their various models, improvements, and design changes. Serious collectors of the American double gun find the lesser-known makers equally interesting, although little information on the gun or makers is available.

One of the "lesser lights" from this period was the Syracuse Arms Company gun (1893–1904). Examples of this interesting gun often exhibit differences that result in confusion to the collector. In fact, these changes actually represent improvements to the original Hollenbeck design and occurred over the course of production for various reasons previously mentioned. The purpose of this essay is to list and illustrate these modifications and to identify the various models noted to date.

Researchers of the Syracuse gun are unlikely to encounter many examples before realizing that significant differences exist between lower and higher serial-numbered guns. These modifications occurred at two points during the production life of the gun. The first change provided additional strength in key areas of stress, the second change improved Hollenbeck's original patent for a hammerless-gun lock mechanism; but, more importantly, these significant modifications were intended to increase appeal among consumers with a lot of options. These two modifications required alteration of the gun frame resulting in three distinct frame variations, which from this point forward will be referenced as the "First Model," the "Second Model," and the "Third Model." These differences are important because they served to improve the gun, and also because they establish the period of manufacture. In addition, anyone contemplating the restoration of a Syracuse gun will realize that certain major components from one model (the barrels for example) cannot be fitted to another model. Making these guns even more interesting are the existence of a few specimens exhibiting combined early- and late-production features. In my opinion, these "hybrids" are anomalies and cannot be designated as a specific model variation; therefore their discussion will be deferred to a more appropriate time.

All Syracuse Arms Company guns are box-frame (boxlock) guns. A distinctive feature of the Syracuse is the frame-to-stock joint. Rather than the typical vertical, straight joint at this point, the Syracuse gun exhibits a sharp angle away from the breech-balls towards the opening lever.

A trio of high-grade examples from the Syracuse Arms Company, along with a rare early Syracuse Arms pocket catalogue. Beginning at the top of the photo the guns represent the following grades: a late-production "B" Grade 12 bore with "Best English Damascus" barrels; a low-numbered "C" Grade 12 bore with Krupps fluid steel barrels; and a "D" Grade 16 bore with Whitworth fluid steel barrels. Respective list prices of these guns in 1902 were $175, $325, and $475; and each grade exhibits progressively finer checkering and carving as well as more elaborate metal sculpting and engraving. Note the frame side profiles of the Grade "B" and Grade "D" as compared to the Grade "C." The radius on the "C" Grade extends to the barrel flats, while the radius on the Grades "B" and "D" ends approximately halfway. This treatment to the frame sides is cosmetic only and was limited to Grades "B", "C", and "D" during production of the "Third Model" (guns above 32xxx).

This was not intended as a cosmetic touch, but was necessary to acquire adequate metal in which to secure the sear pin. This profile was not unique to the Syracuse, as several examples of guns utilizing the Baker gun cocking and bolting mechanism are known to exist. These guns are easily identifiable from the Syracuse by simply examining the frame sides and barrel lug. Syracuse guns (Hollenbeck's patent) will have two visible pins on each side and a 5/8-inch-wide barrel lug. Guns built on the Baker system will have three visible pins on the frame side and a narrower (3/8-inch-wide) barrel lug.

All Syracuse gun frames were steel forgings described as "made from the highest quality of gun metal and, therefore, guaranteed to stand the strain of the nitro powders." At this time I am unable to state the source for the frame forgings, although it is entirely possible that the Baker Gun and Forging Company could have been the supplier. Clearly, steel forgings were a major portion of their business; and Frank Hollenbeck, who had worked for three years prior to forming the Syracuse Arms Company as superintendent of the Baker Gun and Forging Company, could have used his connections to secure the necessary forgings. Additional evidence seems apparent in the box-frame Baker guns and trade-name guns produced by Baker with similar frames. From photos in early mail-order catalogues, it is obvious that Syracuse and Syracuse "look-alike" guns were produced concurrently. Why Baker did so, *if* indeed they also produced frame forgings for Syracuse Arms, is not known, but Syracuse Arms did enjoy some fair success and such attempt, *if* made, could have been to capitalize on that success with a "copy." More study is required in this area.

Among the three model variations, the "First Model" is the most common. This variation represented Frank Hollenbeck's original design and, with the exception of the incorporation of George Horne's patented ejector system in 1896 and an undated forend fastener modification at

Another cosmetic difference between very early and later guns marked "HOLLENBECK" is that the earliest examples feature the gun name and maker in an unmatted panel on the top rib. This information was relocated to the trigger plate very soon after production began.

On facing page: The very early Syracuse Arms Company guns were named and marked "THE HOLLENBECK" after the inventor, Frank H. Hollenbeck. Contrary to thinking by some collectors, guns marked "THE HOLLENBECK" and guns marked "THE SYRACUSE" are not different models, but there are some cosmetic differences. The most obvious of these is the triggerguard contour. Very early examples of "HOLLENBECK" marked guns have guards very similar to other guns of the period. Later "HOLLENBECK" marked guns and all "SYRACUSE" marked guns are fitted with a guard which appears elongated and "flattened." This guard contributed much to providing a unique appearance to the Syracuse gun.

some point shortly afterwards, remained unchanged until 1902. First Model guns will be serial numbered from No. 1 up to approximately No. 245xx, with the highest-recorded First Model example being No. 24631 and the lowest-recorded Second Model example being gun No. 24727. Undoubtedly, some overlap does exist, as I have recorded one early four-digit frame featuring a combination of both First and Third Model characteristics. The fact that some period makers did not pull serialized frames from the parts bin in sequential order was established previously by other researchers; so such example is not startling. Besides, why would a cost-conscious Yankee industrialist type throw away a perfectly good frame, even if dated, when it could possibly be utilized?

First Model examples are easily identified by simply opening the guns and visually examining the rib extension. All Syracuse Arms Company guns, whether marked "THE HOLLENBECK" or "THE SYRACUSE," are top bolted utilizing a crossbolt through the rib extension. Rib extensions on the First Model guns will contain a single, rectangular milled slot to receive the crossbolt. Other differences between the First Model and the Second Model exist in the top strap and at the juncture of the stock head to the frame. First Model guns are constructed with a top strap noticeably shorter and narrower than their counterparts on Second Model examples; and the stock head on First Model guns are fitted flush with the frame, as opposed to Second Model examples, which are inletted into the frame sides to reduce the possibility of splitting. One other visual difference is the safety slide, which was lengthened and reshaped (flattened) to present a more streamlined profile.

The earliest First Model examples of Syracuse Arms Company guns will be marked "THE HOLLENBECK" either on the top rib or on the trigger plate and are seen to approximately SN 5xxx (the highest recorded example to date is No. 4555). The only differences between these guns and the earliest examples of guns marked "THE SYRACUSE" are cosmetic.

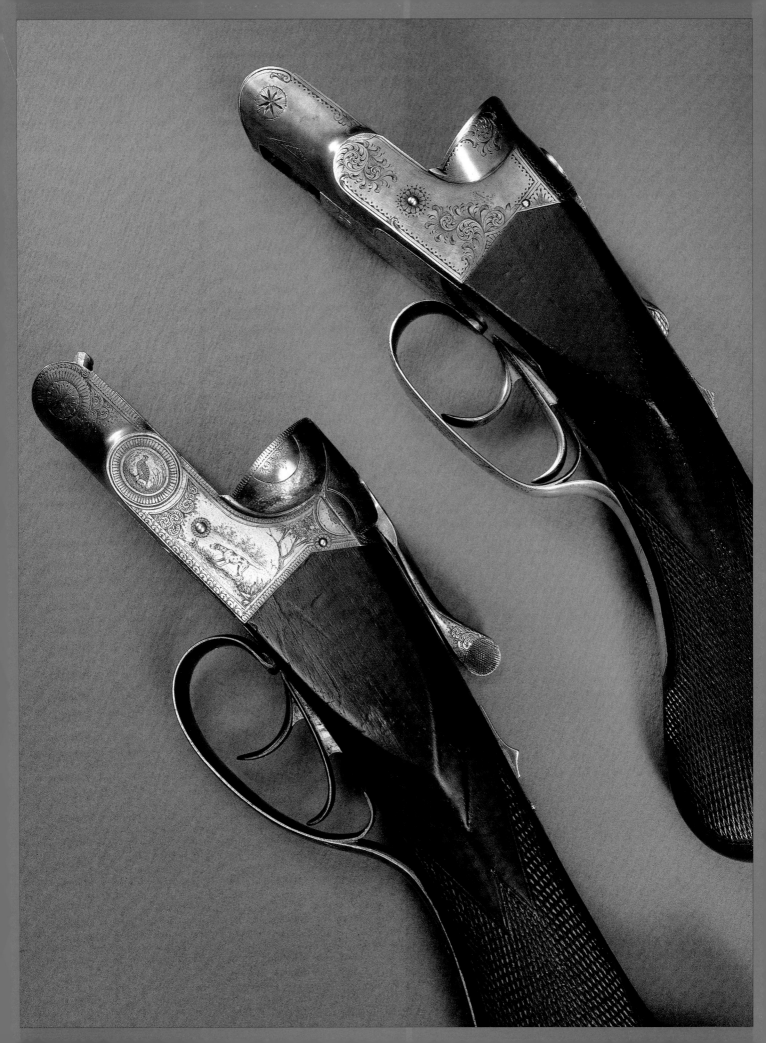

The very first guns marked "THE HOLLENBECK" feature a "rounded" triggerguard typical in appearance to those of other period makers. Early into production, the guard profile was "flattened" and given an elongated appearance, a feature providing much of the unique "look" associated with all Syracuse guns. Other cosmetic changes involved reshaping the forend wood and changing the hard-rubber buttplate design. Syracuse Arms Company buttplates are interesting in that this standard equipment component changed three times over the course of gun production.

The early guns marked "THE HOLLENBECK" (serial numbers 1–4999), regularly shipped with a beautiful "dog's-head" style hard-rubber plate. The dog appeared to be a setter in an oval bordered by the maker's name, "SYRACUSE ARMS CO. SYRACUSE N.Y." The heel and toe were smooth and the surfaces between the outside edge borders and the dog scene were checkered. Evidence seems to indicate that buttplate standards changed in 1896 concurrently with the name change from "THE HOLLENBECK" to "THE SYRACUSE." The new buttplate design featured a solid checkered surface void of maker's name and outdoor scenes and remained the standard until the introduction of the Second Model. Although it is entirely possible that some early guns marked "THE SYRACUSE" were produced with the "dog's-head" buttplates to exhaust available parts, all First Model examples to date marked "THE SYRACUSE" have plain checkered buttplates. Why management elected to change buttplates with the name change is unknown.

Buttplate design was changed again sometime in 1902 with the introduction of the improved Second Model. The new buttplate now exhibited a large smooth area at the heel and toe, while the mid-surface area received a series of opposing diagonal lines, the intersection of which created a single large "diamond" design in the center. Occasionally, a large framed example, with correspondingly substantial stock wood requiring a larger buttplate, will exhibit double "diamonds" in the diagonal line pattern. Again, this change took place around serial number 245xx and continued through the end of production. One interesting observation regarding the various butt-plate styles is that Third Model plates utilized an entirely different mounting screw.

As previously stated, the Second Model was introduced in 1902. Preceding its introduction was a change to a more aggressive marketing strategy to include bold advertising in all period sporting and trade publications with plans to successfully market "THE SYRACUSE" gun nationwide. To meet anticipated "pent-up" demand, factory capacity was expanded and production increased dramatically. A large, flashy newly expanded catalogue (the company's most complete ever published) was made available to promote in great detail its complete product line and announce its re-entry into the high-grade gun trade.

Another cosmetic difference between the early "HOLLEN-BECK" and "SYRACUSE" marked guns is seen in the standard hard-rubber buttplates. All original examples marked "HOLLENBECK" observed to date are fitted with a very nice "dog's-head" style buttplate, covering serial numbers to approximately 5000. It appears that the buttplate design was changed concurrently with the gun name change from Hollenbeck to Syracuse for some unknown reason. The new buttplate (middle) featured a fully checkered surface and was standard from its introduction until 1902 (around serial number 245xx) when the improved "Second Model" was introduced. This redesigned (right side) buttplate featured smooth heel and toe surfaces with a series of diagonal lines intersecting in the middle to form a flat "diamond" checkered pattern. This buttplate was standard on all "Second and Third Model" Syracuse guns through the end of production. Occasionally an example will surface with a factory original extra-thick buttplate (top) used to adjust LOP to a customer's requirement. "First" and "Second" style buttplates utilized identical screws, although their location was altered and length adjusted for buttplate thickness, but the "Third" style buttplate utilized entirely different screws.

The final cosmetic difference between very early guns marked "HOLLENBECK" and later Hollenbeck and Syracuse guns was the shape of the forend wood, which was slightly shortened and narrowed at the tip. The left-most example is from an early, pre-ejector Hollenbeck. The example in the middle is from a very early "SYRACUSE" marked gun produced shortly after the name of the gun was changed and ejectors became standard on Grades "A" and "B." Early guns with ejectors are easily identified by the external retaining screw at the base of the forend. The right-most example is from a later-production Syracuse (Second and Third Models) fitted with ejectors and the ejector on/off switch, a feature standard on "A" and higher grades of the period and optional on lower grades.

"The Syracuse Arms Co: Model Variation" will continue with part 4, in the Winter 2003 issue.

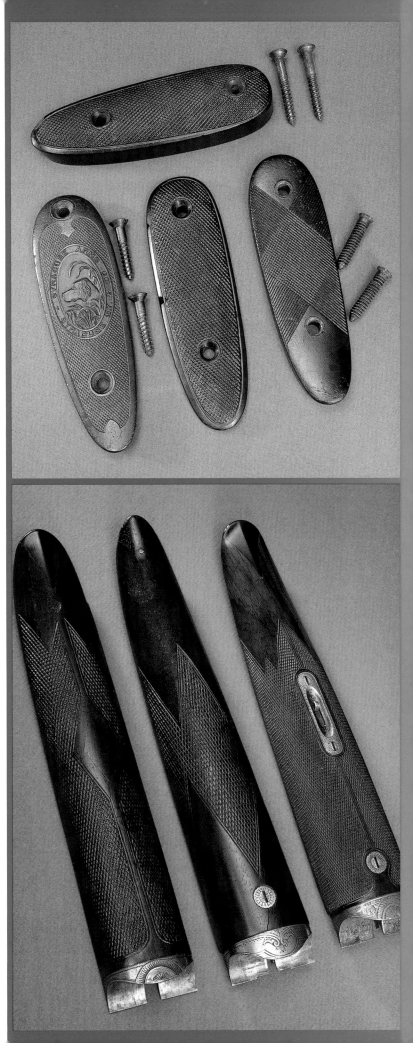

BERETTA

HUMAN WILDLIFE.

NEW YORK   DALLAS   PARIS   BUENOS AIRES   MILANO

Ithaca Crass Model
The Grade 4 With Sculpted Fences

*Written and Photographed
by James T. Tyson*

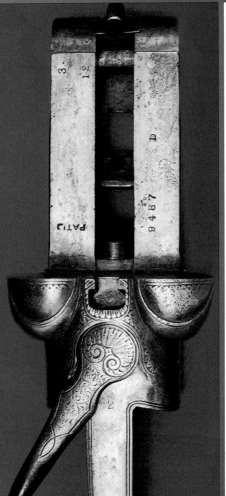

P erhaps the most magnificent guns that the Ithaca Gun Co. ever produced were the Crass Models with sculpted breech balls in Grades 3 and 4 hammerless, and in Grade C or higher hammer gun. There might be a higher-grade gun of this type, but so far, the Grade 4 hammerless is the highest-graded gun bearing the sculpted fences that we know of.

We also know from research provided in Walt Snyder's latest book, *The Ithaca Gun Co: From The Beginning*, that there were 522 hammerless guns made during that first year of production in 1888, and 755 in 1889, for a total of 1307 in all grades of which most were Grades 1, 1½, and 2.

A recently discovered sculpted frame provides us with interesting facts as to the serial range and time this feature was introduced.

This early frame came to me from a man who had it tucked away along with some other Ithaca parts for 30 years. It was most certainly engraved by Joseph Loy. The "ditto" marks after the scroll engraving are typical.

Loy's engraving style became more interesting as time progressed, although engraving patterns were still in the experimental stages when number 9487 was finished. For example, the later Grade 3 guns displayed much more definition in their game scenes.

The lowest number that I have knowledge of is this Grade 3 frame, serial number 9487 hammerless 12 gauge, marked as a number 2 size under

Above and at left: The early Crass frame that helped me identify the beginning of the sculpted features. The "ditto" marks with scroll are a sure indication that Joseph Loy engraved this action body.
On facing page, center: The style of the engraved dog and surrounding work is undoubtably that of Joseph Loy.
Bottom: The letters "SS" are stamped on the forearm.

the top lever. This sculpted breech ball frame dates to the latter part of 1889. In his book, Walt Snyder featured a hammerless gun without these features having serial number 8167, made in late 1888. Therefore we may conclude that almost a year went by in hammerless production before Ithaca decided to introduce sculpted breech ball guns in early 1889. By mid-1892 after about three and a half years in business, with serial numbers in the upper 19000s, to include my gun No. 19570 in Grade 4 , this feature was discontinued.

According to Walt Snyder, the original patent for hammerless guns was filed on May 11, 1889, by Charles Pierce and Leroy Smith. There were also notes about the sliding safety being subject to considerable patent activity. He states, "Three new patents followed in quick succession." My Grade 4 has what I believe to be these new patent numbers stamped on its water table: They are April 10, 1888; May 23, 1888; March 9, 1889. The company catalogues of the era describe Quality No. 4 as having "very fine Damascus barrels, fine selected English walnut stock, pistol grip, checkered, and very finely engraved No. 10, 12, or 16 gauge, $100." None of my Ithaca catalogues show pictures of the sculpted breech ball feature, nor mention it. I have not seen any old magazine articles describing the feature either. These are mysterious specimens to say the least.

These guns are scarce, and unfortunately we have very little information on them since the factory records were destroyed in a fire. There

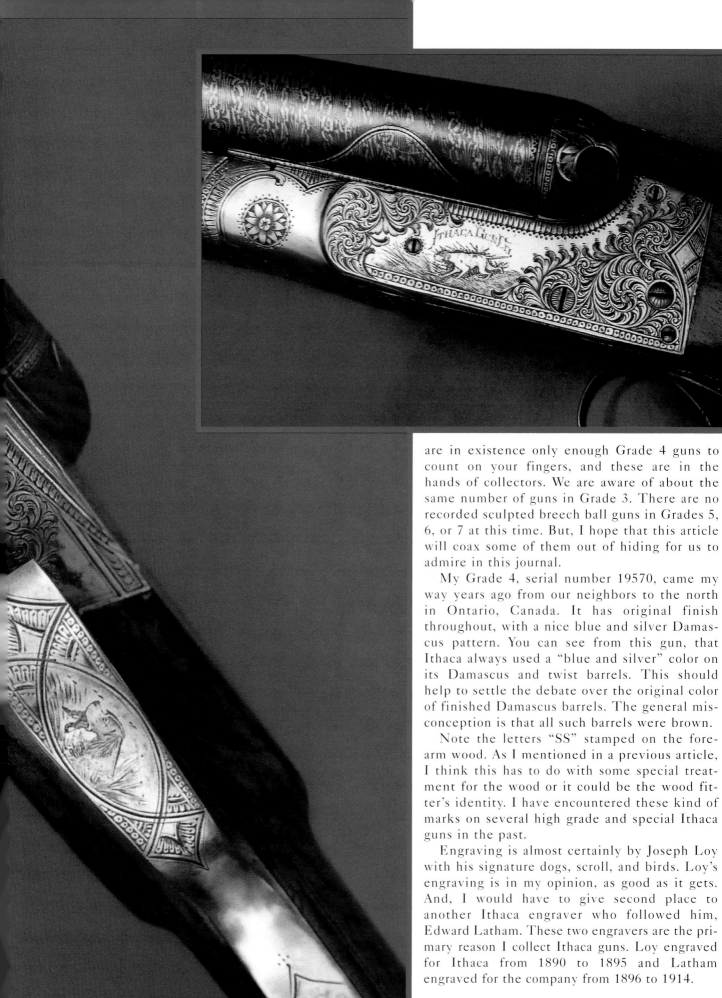

are in existence only enough Grade 4 guns to count on your fingers, and these are in the hands of collectors. We are aware of about the same number of guns in Grade 3. There are no recorded sculpted breech ball guns in Grades 5, 6, or 7 at this time. But, I hope that this article will coax some of them out of hiding for us to admire in this journal.

My Grade 4, serial number 19570, came my way years ago from our neighbors to the north in Ontario, Canada. It has original finish throughout, with a nice blue and silver Damascus pattern. You can see from this gun, that Ithaca always used a "blue and silver" color on its Damascus and twist barrels. This should help to settle the debate over the original color of finished Damascus barrels. The general misconception is that all such barrels were brown.

Note the letters "SS" stamped on the forearm wood. As I mentioned in a previous article, I think this has to do with some special treatment for the wood or it could be the wood fitter's identity. I have encountered these kind of marks on several high grade and special Ithaca guns in the past.

Engraving is almost certainly by Joseph Loy with his signature dogs, scroll, and birds. Loy's engraving is in my opinion, as good as it gets. And, I would have to give second place to another Ithaca engraver who followed him, Edward Latham. These two engravers are the primary reason I collect Ithaca guns. Loy engraved for Ithaca from 1890 to 1895 and Latham engraved for the company from 1896 to 1914.

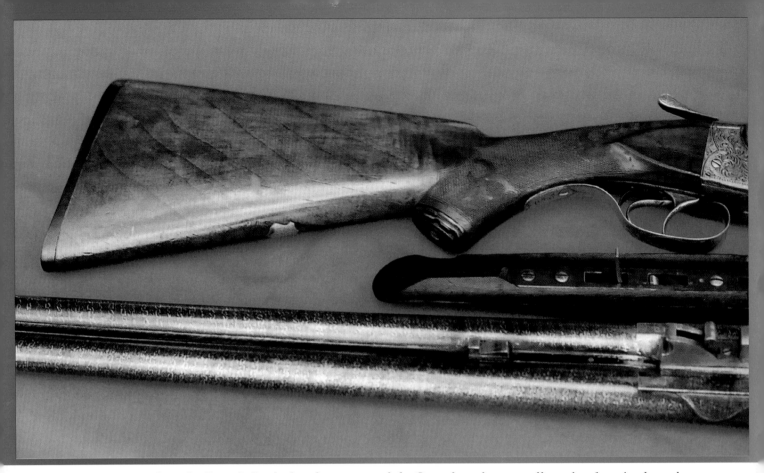

The Damascus barrels, fleur-de-lis checkered pattern and the Crass buttplate are all works of art in themselves.

I am including a letter from the DeWitt Historical Society in Ithaca, New York, showing a list of engravers and the dates they were employed by Ithaca. Loy is first listed in the city directories in 1890 and last mentioned in the 1894–1895 directory. He didn't move to Ilion, New York, until after 1894.

Another interesting engraver is Emille Guilment, listed in the 1890–1891 directory with the same address as Joseph Loy. Some of the mystery guns might have been engraved by him under the supervision of Loy.

Robert Runge, Sr., engraved Ithaca guns from 1905 to 1906 and was another good engraver who then went to work for Remington. I might mention at this time how much I enjoy all the articles and the excellent book entitled *Remington Double Shotguns*, by fellow *DGJ* author Charles Semmer, which portrays outstanding engraving on early Remington doubles by these aforementioned artists.

I have some beautiful engraved Remington rifles in my collection that remind me of Remington's dedication to quality. Simeon Rogers engraved at Ithaca from 1919 to 1920 and is another craftsman who was lost to Remington employment.

Percy Clapp was listed as an engraver from 1901 to 1932. I believe he must have been one of those engravers Jay Leech mentioned, "He sat by me and was an engraver of line and border work up to Grade 1 or 2 after which the master engraver took over for the game scenes."

With a lineup of engravers such as this, no one can deny that the Ithaca Gun Company shipped some of the most masterfully engraved guns in the history of gunmaking.

The DeWitt Historical Society *of* **Tompkins County**
Tompkins County Museum ❖ Eight Square Schoolhouse
401 East State Street, Ithaca, New York 14850
(607) 273-8284 Fax: (607) 273-6107

June 18, 2002

Mr. James T. Tyson
2670 Co. Rd. 63
Tuskegee, AL 36083

Dear Mr. Tyson:

Thank you very much for your recent letter and the check for the research fee. As far as the rest of your questions are concerned, I hope the following information is helpful:
(First I need to mention that all our information has come from city directories. We do not have an 1890 census. Maybe you could get information from it on the internet?)
First, **Emille Guilmont** is listed only in the 1890-1891 directory, and none of the others, either before or after.
Joseph Loy is first listed in the 1890-1891 directory, and the last listing for him is in the 1894-1895 directory.
Edward Latham (in the directories it's spelled "**Laytham**") is first mentioned in the 1896-1897 directory, and the last listing is in the 1913-1914 volume. In each he is listed as an "engraver" only.
Robert Runge, interestingly, is only listed in the 1905-1906 directory ("emp gun works, bds 201 E. Yates").
Simeon Rogers also has only one listing, in the 1919-1920 directory as an engraver, living at 409 Linn St.
I couldn't find a listing for **Jack Clance** at all.
Percy Clapp was listed in every directory from 1901 until 1932. He's either listed as an "engraver" or a "gun engraver" throughout most of the years, except at the end, when he was probably retired. From 1929 on he's listed only with an address. And after 1932 he's not listed at all. His addresses vary from 209 N. Plain, to 404 Cascadilla, to 521 N. Albany, to 815 N. Tioga, to 413 W. Buffalo St.
I hope that takes care of your questions. I spent a little over two hours on this research, and at $15. per hour that makes the further charge $30.
Thank you again for your lovely donation of the Double Gun Journals, and thank you for thinking of the DeWitt for your research needs. If we can be of further service, please don't hesitate to get in touch again.

Sincerely yours,

Donna Eschenbrenner
Archivist

BOSS & CO. LTD.
MAKERS OF BEST GUNS ONLY

Gun and Rifle Makers

16 Mount Street
London, W1

Boss & Co Stock			
Pair Boss & Co			
12 Bore Round Body	Side by Side	28" S/T	Ref: 0149
Pair Boss & Co			
12 Bore Round Body	Side by Side	27" S/T	Ref: 0088
Pair Boss & Co			
12 Bore Square Body	Side by Side	29" S/T	Ref: 0092
Pair Boss & Co			
12 Bore Square Body	Side by Side	28" S/T	Ref: 0101
Pair Boss & Co			
16 Bore Round Body	Side by Side	28" S/T	Ref: 1038
Pair Boss & Co			
16 Bore Square Body	Side by Side	28" S/T	Ref: 0089
Boss & Co			
12 Bore Square Body	Over & Under	29" S/T	Ref: 0152
Boss & Co			
12 Bore Pigeon	Over & Under	29" S/T	Ref: 0102
Boss & Co			
12 Bore Square Body	Over & Under	29" S/T	Ref: 0158
Boss & Co			
12 Bore Square Body	Over & Under	29" S/T	Ref: 0181
Boss & Co			
12 Bore Square Body	Side by Side	29" S/T	Ref: 0040
Boss & Co			
12 Bore Square Body	Side by Side	29" S/T	Ref: 0002
Boss & Co			
12 Bore Square Body	Side by Side	27"/29" S/T	Ref: 491
Boss & Co			
12 Bore Square Body	Side by Side	29" S/T	Ref: 0061
Boss & Co			
12 Bore Square Body	Side by Side	29" S/T	Ref: 0125

Boss & Co			
20 Bore Square Body	Side by Side	28" S/T	Ref: 0054
Boss & Co			
20 Bore Round Body	Side by Side	28" S/T	Ref: 0130
Swaine & Adney			
20 Bore Square Body	Side by Side	28" D/T	Ref: 0176
Watson Bros			
20 Bore Round Body	Side by Side	29" D/T	Ref: 0177
Webley and Scott			
20 Bore Boxlock	Ejector	28" D/T	Ref: 0195
Purdey			
20 Bore Square Body	Side by Side	28" D/T	Ref: 0085
Purdey			
12 Bore Pigeon	Side by Side	28" S/T	Ref: 0124
Pair Churchill			
12 Bore "Hercules"	Side by Side	28" D/T	Ref: 0154
Holland			
12 Bore "Sporting"	Over & Under	31" S/T	Ref: 0135
Holland			
12 Bore "Northwood"	Side by Side	28" D/T	Ref: 0144
Holland			
16 Bore "Northwood"	Side by Side	28" D/T	Ref: 0163
Holland			
20 Bore "Northwood"	Side by Side	28" D/T	Ref: 0164
Thos Adsett			
.410 Boxlock	Ejector	28" D/T	Ref: 0167

WANTED good examples of Boss & Co.
Also other English makes of sporting Sidelock or Boxlock guns in good condition. Fair prices paid, immediate decisions made.
All Guns covered by Boss & Co Warranty
Boss Gunmakers Ltd, 16 Mount Street, London W1K 2HR England
Telephone: +44(0)20 7493 1127   Facsimile: +44(0)20 7493 0711
www.Bossguns.com

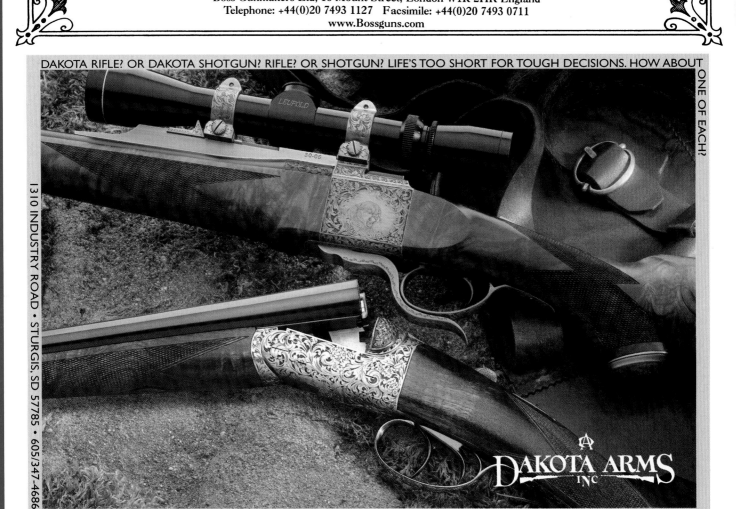

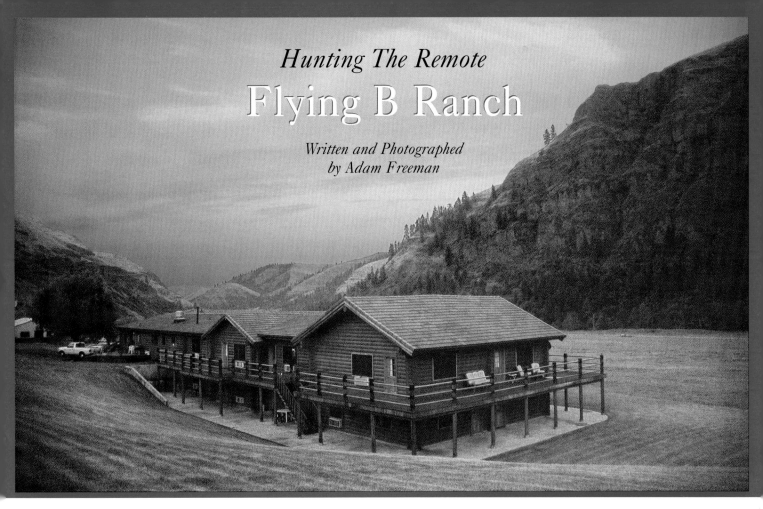

Hunting The Remote
Flying B Ranch

*Written and Photographed
by Adam Freeman*

For some time I have heard about a large, comfortable and secluded lodge nestled in a remote Idaho canyon, full of Lewis and Clark history and western charm, where the bird hunting is never slow and the stable full of dogs beyond compare...

I awoke just as we entered Lawyer Canyon, and once on the property, I began to see bird cover everywhere I looked. It is planted all the way up and down the six miles of the canyon property, down the bottomlands alongside the rocky, blue- and whitewater Lawyer Creek and up on the sides of the orange lava rock cliffs. The perfect bird cover was everywhere, in fact over the past twenty years the owner of the property has annually planted the hills with snowberries, and Russian olives, and wheat, and rye to name but a few.

Arriving at the spacious and impressive log lodge, I was welcomed by a hot blazing fire in a grand stone hearth, friendly faces and welcoming hors d'oeuvres and soon a quiet room and a large comfortable bed.

The following morning, after a delicious breakfast, I was ready to get on with some bird shooting.

Ray (my guide) with super dogs, Bar and Banker.

Banker, a stout two-year-old pointer of Elhew descent, who came from a litter with siblings named Money and Cash, hunted with true gusto, charging on like a bull market almost as if he were eager to get some sort of lucrative deal. Bar, who would soon become one of my favorites was a five-year-old German shorthair.

Eventually reaching the hunting fields, we worked away from the truck, cutting across the wind. Bar, Banker, and my guide Ray, waited patiently for me to bring up the rear with my excess equipment. Ray cast a contemptuous eye at me as I fumbled with camera and sketching pad, clumsily trying to fit a Dakota Arms 28 gauge into the soup.

We then began to make some progress towards our mutual goals. The strong flowing whitewater of Lawyer Creek lay ahead with plenty of sharp-edged grassy bird haunts between us. Multiple dried up rock beds peppered the bottomland fields and the dogs knew to check them for scent. The rocks that choked the dried up beds just happened to be about the size and color of an adult chukar! Five minutes out Bar got bedrock birdie! Shaking his tail, his gate swinging left then right then back left, his head rising and

falling, he magically turned into a pose that deserved to be carved in marble. Immediately noticing Bar's lockup, Banker honored him. Converging on the would-be birds hidden somewhere in the rocks we all eased up, straining our eyes in an effort to find them before they burst for the sky. Ray spotted one first, a lone rock-impersonating chukar hunkered down, head held low in the rocks and just as I got my camera up, that fat chalky-gray bird shot up as if out of a cannon. I decided to take a much closer look at the rocks in the bed! Bob West and his father-in-law Bob Fouser both swung on the bird; one or both of them dropping him. It only took a

At top: Three of the five shotguns I used. From top: Dakota Arms Legend Grade in 28 gauge, Dakota Arms Premier Grade in 16 gauge, and the Charles Hellis Premier in 12 bore.

few more steps and Banker, who was running full bore, hit the emergency brakes and swung hard struggling to lock up as his momentum carried him forward, his claws raking the ground tearing out grass and throwing up dust. He kept his balance impressing us all with his tenacity toward the game. Bar was busy in the high grass bordering a small, waist-high washout complete with bird-size caves behind exposed roots. We were shortly faced with a lovely problem, two dogs on point.

Once we reached the tangled cover near the creek we got into some rooster pheasant all vying for a lady on their small patches of turf. Here I substituted my camera for the graceful little Dakota 28 bore. Rising up and over the rock floodwall that bordered the creek, Banker disappeared on the opposite side, his bell around his neck falling silent. I carefully climbed up the wall. There was Banker shaking with excitement and waiting on point watching a full bloom rooster pheasant running through the thick underbrush dodging the leafless limbs. Crouching down watching that rooster scoot away and not even able to do anything about it, I noticed Bar on the other side of the rock wall. He was a good 90 yards

es he turned and headed over the water. I leveled off that graceful 28 and missed, then the second barrel cracked and folded nothing but my confidence in my ability as a solid game shot. I suppose I had had too much time to think about how easy this bird would be. Neither of those fine dogs gave me a scolding look, not the case with Ray and the others. We walked the edge of the clear Lawyer Creek, three wide, two with guns, and watched the dogs work. Swinging back toward the truck I elected to walk through the heavier cover with the "boys" as they worked every angle trying to find more birds to add to our heavy bag. Finding the truck through the brush was never hard; I could hear the other dogs bawling in anguish wanting their turn

distant. The wind wafting in Banker's face and mine was not in Bar's favor. I think he had just simply seen this routine before, and knew what to do next; there was no way possible he could have seen this rooster or Banker and only my head and shoulders showed above the rocks. He suddenly changed his course heading into the direction I was looking. In one bound he was atop the rock wall. He knew the bird could only be one place since there was no scent in his location, not even residual—the bird had not had time to travel that far. Whatever the case, Bar's rear end almost went over his head as he topped that wall and tried to lock up on rolling rock. Like bookends, those two dogs trapped that cagey old bird. Nowhere left to go but up through the snarling clutter of interlocked limbs, that rooster flushed almost getting trapped in the process. Breaking free of the bush-

at hunting. We loaded up Bar and Banker, bloody toed from the rocks, and I slipped them a treat from my pocket for a first-rate performance. It was time for a rest for them.

The weather continued to be perfect for picking up bird scent. This is tough country and the dirt roads we traveled were etched deeply with ruts from previous hunting parties. We were headed up to Stillman, its reputation for spectacular views preceding it. Stillman consists of several easy to hunt semi-flat plateaus at various ascending altitudes ending at around 2200 feet.

Briar, a large German shorthair with a gray muzzle, a bowed back and the eyes and nose of a dog who has found and held over 50,000 birds, was our next hunting companion. He is twelve and has been hunting birds in this country better than six months a year for all of those twelve years.

As I was loading my gear I turned around to see Briar on point right out of the truck. I wondered, were there more birds up here on Stillman or was Briar's experience the difference?

He worked a little slower than the others but I imagine he saw no solid reason to hurry. It was a treat to watch a master of birds doing his job. Easing up the sloping plateau with Briar bringing up the rear, we turned around to see the wise one on point casting a disapproving eye up at us. He was solid and confident on a rooster pheasant that we had just walked past! Creeping up on him, we noticed the iridescent bird in a thick tangle at the base of several wiry saplings. The bird was holding tight. Two veterans playing an old

rocketing bird, not a muscle moving! Bob Fouser swatted that old warrior pheasant and the cloud of feathers that rained down on Briar mattered not as he fetched up what was left of his adversary. We pushed on, hunting over Briar till he tired.

Out with the deadly duo again, Bar and Banker sprang from their boxes. With the enthusiasm of two pups hunting for the first time, they tore up the steep hill that shadowed us. They topped the rocky crest and disappeared. I started up after them and nearly ten minutes later crested the jagged edge that took them all of a minute to clear. There they were twenty feet away on top of a small bluff under some pines. They had gone no further than this when Banker

game, holding their own ground waiting for the other to show his hand. Well, when that big rooster saw us easing up, enlightened as we were by Briar's nose, he must have thought the jig was up. He exploded from his sheltered cubbyhole with all the chatter and power he could scrape together. I will never hold it against Briar for closing his eyes when that wing slapped his face and I will never forget him looking up at the

The bird hunting emphasis is on Huns, although there is a large population of pheasant, chukar, quail, and ruffed and blue grouse. On facing page, these Hungarian partridge were harvested using, from left: Lefever Arms Co., F.P. Baker & Co., and the Charles Hellis of London.

locked up on point and Bar honored him. For nearly ten minutes they held point. Lucky for them I also cradled the Dakota double. After a few snapshots with the camera, I surmised I would finish what that rooster had started. I managed to add that bird to my gamebag.

We were soon amazed once again by Bar. He was running alongside a rather steep hill completely covered with very loose small rocks. He suddenly locked up on

For the shooter and non-shooter alike, fish the middle branch of the Clearwater River, or take pack-in horseback trips to fish for trout, to hunt small and big game, or to admire the awesome beauty of the high country and alpine lakes.

point and then quickly began to slide down the hill. He never broke point or lost his balance! Banker honored this sliding point looking puzzled through the whole incident and relieved when it ended.

We finished off a perfect day in the field and headed down off Stillman with dozens of birds in the bag and a few easily forgotten misses. Back at the warm, inviting lodge a lovely dinner of prime rib awaited us.

The next morning the weather again promised to be a comfortable day though just a bit warm for a dog's nose. I was stationed with the Spezios and they were headed into the far side of the bottoms where I hunted the first leg

At top: The Dakota Arms Legend Model 28 bore. The gun's rounded body is reminiscent of Dickson and MacNaughton, but the action is based on Anson & Deeley. The barrels are chopper-lump and the firing pins disc-striker. The trigger system is very unique. The front trigger on a two-trigger gun is actually able to fire both barrels with no complex selection procedure. All the while, the rear trigger will still fire the left barrel, providing the best of both worlds!

out. Our guide was Rich Coe and his dog Cy. We also had the rare treat of hunting over Sass, who happens to be Jerry Cross's personal dog. Jerry is the trainer and breeder of all those wonderful dogs. Along with his dog-training duties, Jerry also oversees the bird management with over 100,000 birds annually. Sass is a very small shorthair with a very large heart, a real hunter. The other team was DJ and Bravo. Both were known among this remarkable group for their long noses. Rich brought the truck to a moaning stop just as we entered the field. "OK, let's hunt," he said.

Little did I know that he planned to take us up one of those slight mountains at the end of our bird march through the field. Those rock-riddled slopes with their thick moss-burdened gnarly bushes were over-populated with some wild old birds of multiple species. Sass and Cy ripped those bottom fields apart locking up repeatedly in perfect pose. By the time we reached the end of the field we were forced to empty our game bags. Rich went back for the truck in order to ford the creek and bring on fresh dogs. That done, up we went. Walking up an old shadowy trail that weaved its way through the ancient wall of brush made it difficult to keep track of the dogs. If they went on point I was not sure how we could do anything about it. Rich however knew how this was to work, so did the fresh reserves Bravo and DJ. Two other hunters were positioned two hundred yards below our path. Rich, Mark Spezio, and I took the steep trail less traveled!

Bravo and DJ worked a technique that must have taken awhile to learn. They pinched that hill between them. Bravo stayed up high while DJ hunted down in the thick stuff between the lower hunters and us. The shooting was very fast; you never knew when or where the birds would come up. Bravo

Author Adam Freeman–
a long way from Cincinnati.

would simply point them from the trail so we could see her looking down into the tangles. These birds would not sit long with a heavy pointer busting through the bush. If they headed downhill the shooters below us had a high driven-bird shot. We got into the usual birds as well as a few coveys of California quail and some lively grouse by the time we reached the end of the logging road where the walking became much easier. We dropped down and doubled back picking up some of the missed birds as we went.

That afternoon I elected to head back up to Stillman for my last evening's hunt. I could have gone any number of places that I had yet to see on the 4,200-acre property. I wanted to go back up to Stillman for the view, and if I had my choice I would have been there with Briar. However, Cy and Sass played no second fiddle to any of the other dogs and put on another perfect concert up there.

I can say that I am eager to return to that isolated Idaho canyon one day. No bag limits are imposed there. The birds are plentiful and extremely strong flyers. Some of them flew, some ran and hid and impersonated inanimate objects, but in the end, they could not escape those fantastic dogs!

We're Not Just Talking Tough!
Wear Filson When You Mean It.

Suddenly, the scent turns uphill and you're grabbing for slough grass and solid footing. You'll only get one crack at beating this bird before he launches for the next county!

When the birds turn "bad" you'll be glad you wear Filson. Some build clothes that are rugged. Some build clothes to stay dry. We build clothes for both. At Filson we believe that exceptional durability and protection must be part of every product we make.

Our reputation began more than 100 years ago in the Pacific Northwest when we crafted

clothing to help miners survive the Alaskan Klondike. Our philosophy since the beginning has been – *Build it right the first time or they may not be back* – literally!

Today our products, including our rugged line of upland clothes, are still manufactured in the USA from the best natural materials available. Tightly woven 100% cotton, long fibered

100% virgin wool and genuine bridle leather are unique materials you'll only find in authentic Filson products.

So on your next hunt turn to Filson. You'll be comfortable and protected in the most durable hunting clothing available.

Filson. Plan on us hunting together for the rest of your life.

For the name of the Filson retailer nearest you or a free catalog call 1-800-624-0201, or visit us at www.filson.com. Please mention DG9.

"Might As Well Have The Best"®
FILSON®
◄ Since 1897 ►

THERE is *only* one thing more *satisfying* than owning a *William & Son* shotgun. OWNING a *pair*.

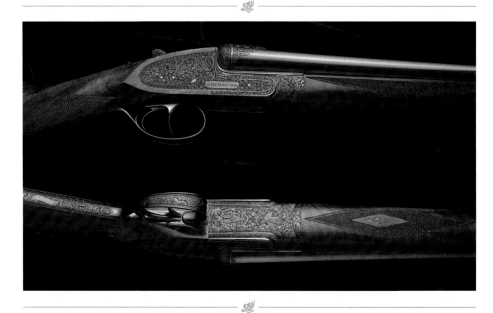

WILLIAM & SON

10 Mount Street London W1K 2TY Tel +44 (0) 20 7493 8385 Fax +44 (0) 20 7493 8386 info@williamandson.com www.williamandson.com

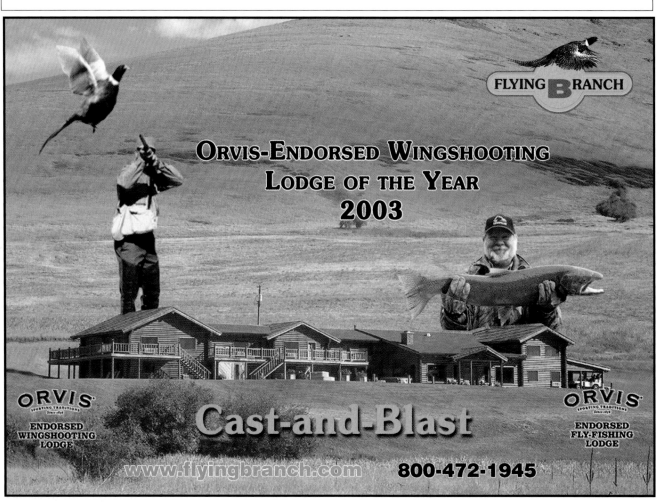

J.P. Sauer & Sohn's
Deutsch Reich Patent No. 78411

Written and Photographed
by Jeff Stephens

Eighteen hundred and ninety-three was a banner year for J.P. Sauer & Sohn of Suhl, as it was also for the relatively young and recently unified German Empire. For Sauer & Sohn it was a year of improvements in the manufacture of their double guns and application for patent protection of a new sidelock drilling gun design. For the Empire, it was the year that saw the implementation of the compulsory proof of small arms from a law enacted by the Reichstag in 1891. As many readers already are aware, prior to 1893 there was no formal requirement for German manufactured firearms to undergo the rigorous requirements imposed on a firearm that occurred during the actual course of proving a shotgun, rifle, or side arm. The new Empire and its elected legislating body had the foresight to enact this new proof law so that German firearm manufacturers were able to compete in world markets with weapons produced by the British, Austrian, and Belgian trades. The proof law avoided the redundant business of having to re-proof a German-made firearm by the importing nation(s) and had the added side benefit of making German-made guns more easily exported to markets around the world.

J.P Sauer & Sohn in 1894 would market their revolutionary new hammerless drilling design to a world eager for new things. This unique and patented design has withstood the test of time and is considered by many collectors and shooters of these weapons to be arguably the best drilling design ever conceived and produced by any manufacturer.

For those readers who are not interested in the more technical aspects of the design feel free to skip to the section regarding the Sauer & Sohn 1907 catalogue. For those who are more mechanically inclined, the effort to read through this section will be informative and will offer the chance to learn something new about an old firearm design produced well over 100 years ago. Patent No. 78411 was applied for on 3 November 1893 at the Kaiser's patent office in Berlin and was granted on 20 December 1894. The document is emblazoned with the Prussian Eagle as will be seen on all official government documents of the era and which would later be seen on virtually all currency minted and or printed during Kaiser Wilhelm II's reign. The drillings themselves are

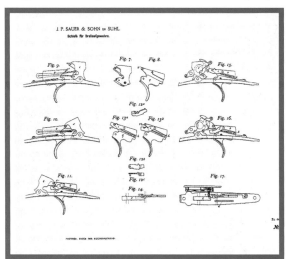

A drawing sheet from Deutsch Reich Patent 78411 illustrating various parts and aspects of the design. This left-side photo illustrates the relative position of the rifle-barrel hammer when it is in the cocked position. Again the more important aspects of the design are between the area of the two triggers and are obscured by the surrounding parts.

easily identified as there is a separate lever located along the left-hand side of the action, exactly where one's thumb would fall if the shooter were right-handed. The lever is somewhat reminiscent of Steven Grant's side-opening levers as found on some of that company's marvelous shotguns but stylistically it is much more compact and efficiently placed. This sidelever as found on Sauer sidecock drillings is used to cock the hammer for the rifle barrel and as a method to switch between this third rifle barrel and the left shotgun barrel.

The approved patent is eight pages long, two pages of which describe the mechanics and six of which illustrate the function and operation of the system. The descriptive prose contained in the pages of the patent is concise and detailed, as one would expect from such a landmark piece of gun design and engineering. The various views that accompany the document are clear and show in detail the way the system works. The illustrations that accompany the patent include standard top or illustrative views along with partial side views of the triggerplate assembly and also of the rifle-barrel hammer, featuring its specially folded rear-extension hook. The rear trigger also features its own folded hook that mechanically engages, or interlocks with the folded hook of the hammer. These two opposing hooks, one on the trigger and one on the hammer are key features of the design and allow the mechanism to function properly with a minimum of parts. The sidelever assembly and its coil-spring-powered yoke assembly is also shown in the drawings. The spring-powered yoke assembly's sole purpose is to provide resistance to the sidelever when it is cycled. The rifle-barrel hammer has its own "V" spring dedicated to powering this hammer, as one would expect. Isometric views are also included in the patent and serve to illustrate the rear trigger, selection/cycling lever, and the rifle-barrel hammer.

The manipulation of the sidelever accomplishes several tasks when it is fully depressed and run through its cycle. The lever serves two primary functions. These two functions are the cocking of the rifle-barrel hammer and as a barrel selector. After the lever is fully depressed the rifle-barrel system is activated and will fire when the rear trigger is pulled. A small post or cocking indicator projecting through the frame, to the rear of the breech and just to the left of the top release lever, shows when the rifle-barrel is cocked and ready to fire. When this indicator is in the "up" or raised position, the rifle-barrel is ready to fire; when in the down position, this post indicates that the rifle hammer has been tripped/fired or has been manually de-cocked.

Initially and as already noted when the sidelever is depressed and run through its complete range, the sidelever cocks the rifle-barrel hammer and enables the rear trigger to release the same. As the specially shaped rifle-barrel ham-

events is reversed. After the firing of the rifle barrel with the rear trigger, by a short stroke of the sidelever, the system is switched back to the left shot barrel. It then becomes possible to fire the left barrel when the rear trigger is pulled.

It must be noted that the ability to fire the right shotgun barrel will always be available—even with the rifle barrel system cocked and engaged. This is a finer point of the system. If one is deer hunting and a shot presents itself at buckshot range it is just a matter of firing the right shot barrel and subsequently following the first shot up with the

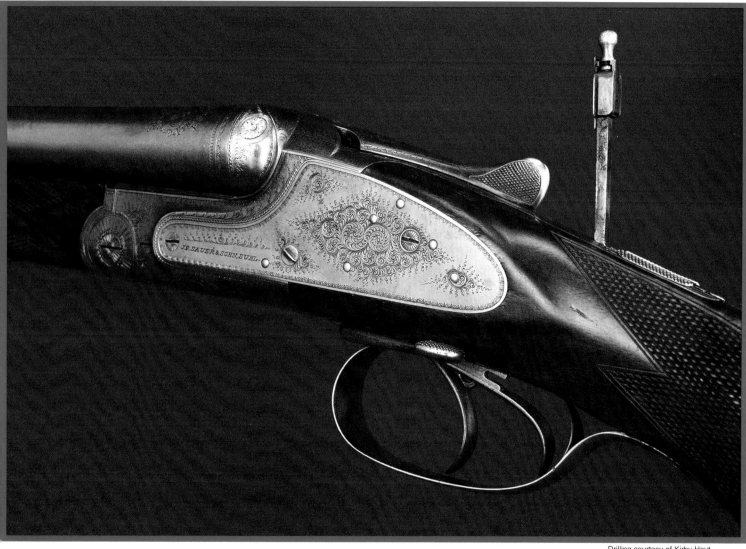

Drilling courtesy of Kirby Hoyt

Sauer & Sohn Model XXV with rear peep sight in upright location. Tang safety is relieved to allow sight to rest flush to top strap of frame on those models equipped with this feature.

mer revolves rearward, a corner or knee at the extreme rear of the hammer contacts and disengages a small lever arm mounted on the upper portion of the front trigger. This small lever arm revolves via a shaft around a fixed point or hole on the trigger sub-assembly and is powered by its own dedicated "feather" spring arm fitted into a milled recess of the trigger sub-assembly. As the rifle-barrel hammer continues through its arc of rotation, two opposing hooks of the rifle-barrel hammer and the trigger sub-assembly subsequently become interlocked and will be released when the rear trigger is pulled. For de-cocking, the sequence of

rifle barrel—if it is needed. This firing of the barrel(s) of course can only occur with the safety in the off position—if it fires with the safety on, get that drilling to a gunsmith and have it fixed!

Another interesting aspect of the design is that if one wishes to de-cock the rifle barrel on a cocked Sauer & Sohn side-cock drilling, the design features the unique ability to control the fall of the rifle-barrel hammer by utilizing the sidelever as a sort of "brake". By pushing the sidelever down with the thumb and holding it, and then activating the rear trigger, the hammer can be let down gently with

thumb pressure retarding the fall of the hammer. This alleviates the concern of dry firing on an empty chamber. Before leaving this subject, a word needs to be said about the assembly of drillings. *Always, Always, Always* pull a drilling's extractor all the way out away from the barrels *before* putting barrels and action together. This will prevent any damage to the extractor slide.

There are no less than four models of side-cocker drillings illustrated in the 1907 JPS&S catalogue. All of them are based on the standard patented design with each model somewhat reminiscent of Steven Grant's fine doubles and includes a Greener crossbolt. The frame on this model is without side clips. Engraving is similar to the Model XXV and it retailed for 400 Marks. The next model, the XXVI was Sauer & Sohn's *Masterwerk* drilling with Greener crossbolt, side clips and featuring profuse scroll engraving, costing 750 Marks. These latter two models, the XXV and the XXVI are seldom found for sale here in the US with only a few known examples among collectors. Sauer's last hammerless drilling illustrated in their 1907 catalogue is the

Model XXV illustrating bushed firing pins. Note the barely visible cross-hatching present on the end of the barrels. This is a finishing touch often found on Sauer guns made for the German domestic market.

having slightly different exterior characteristics, either in engraving patterns and amount of coverage and/or whether or not the gun in question features side clips. The first model illustrated in the hammerless drilling section of the catalogue shows the basic Model XXIV. It shows a nicely appointed drilling with approximately 30 percent engraving coverage and a stippled top whose barrels feature a doll's-head rib extension without a Greener crossbolt and retailing for 300 German Marks. The next model illustrated is the Model XXV with features similar to the Model XXIV except this gun features foliated fences

Model XXVII and it is actually a Model XXV frame with much more engraving and better quality of finish retailing for 500 Marks.

A few words regarding frame types and models follow. In the course of research in preparation for the writing of this article, there appears to have been some hybridization of side-cock drilling models. Specifically the use of the Model XXVI frame with side clips and Greener crossbolt, combined with standard Model XXIV's modest amount of engraving. This model of course is not shown in the 1907 JPS&S catalogue. This example may represent the usage of

Drilling courtesy of Scott King

Trigger-plate view of Daly Model 108. Note the "D.R.P. 78411" engraved just forward of the triggerguard.

available frames drawn from stores, or perhaps this example was a special order piece, knowledgeable collectors just don't know at this time. Regardless of circumstance, the Sauer sidelock side-cock drillings with side clips are exceptionally uncommon here in the United States.

The reader has probably surmised that one will only occasionally come across these J.P. Sauer & Sohn side-cock

drillings. The reasons for their relative scarcity are twofold: One reason is that there is no known catalogue evidence documenting that Schoverling, Daly & Gales or Von Lengerke & Detmold, both of New York, imported these Sauer guns and reason number two, the available examples here in the USA that this author has seen were all made for Germany's domestic market. In other words, the Sauer-

made side-cocker drillings available today in the used-gun market were brought to our shores by returning GI's after the end of WWII.

Sauer & Sohn side-cockers are generally chambered in 16 or 12 gauge with the rifle barrel usually chambered for the 9.3 x 72R cartridge. Other rifle chamberings were also available at the time such as the Winchester 25-35 (6.5 x 52R).

There is currently at least one known side-cock drilling in 16x16 x 9.3x74R, proofed in 1934, but undoubtedly there were others in this configuration as well as those that will be found in 8x57 JRS. The cited 1934 gun bears no similarity in either quality or in frame style to the earlier produced side-cock examples made prior to WWI. It was built using Sauer's second-generation flat-top frame style and features shallow and very modest engraving. It had been thought for some time by this author that side-cock drillings were discontinued in the early to mid-1920s when Sauer came out with the Model XXVa drilling—a hammerless sidelock gun without the separate cocking lever. The XXVa drilling was likely designed sometime after WWI and introduced to the shooting public sometime around 1925. The recent discovery of the aforementioned side-cock drilling built in the mid-1930s did away with the notion that Sauer had stopped production of the side-cocker altogether. This 1934 example shows that the side-cockers were still being built until at least 1934 and probably even later than that. How much later will probably never be known, as there are no known Sauer production records in existence despite continuing rumors to the contrary.

Sauer side-cockers are seldom encountered in 20 gauge but there is at least one known example that was produced. Most, but not all Sauer side-cocker drillings will be fitted with a rear peep sight which folds into the top strap of the receiver. All will have a rear folding leaf sight mounted on the top rib as well as a standard tang-mounted safety. These drillings handle and point like any well made double gun and with the convenience of their standard tang-mounted safety, they are quick in the field for fast flushing game birds.

Weights of Sauer's side-cocker drillings, according to catalogues of the time, varied from 7 pounds 4 ounces to 7 pounds 15 ounces with a stated barrel length of 25 and 7/8 inches. Lighter weights in these guns have been seen, but they are generally only lighter by several ounces. All of the hammerless sidelock side-cocker guns will feature bushed firing pins. Some of the earliest produced models will also feature a "widow's peak" horn buttplate. An interesting and unique type of buttplate occasionally seen on very early Sauer-produced double guns and drillings. Buttstocks on these guns will be pistol-gripped with a steel grip cap or of the round knob, or half-pistol-grip style. The right shot barrel will generally be of fairly open choke, for the "shooting of buck shot" and the left barrel will be bored for "close shooting."

Another well-known name by collectors and shooters of German guns, Charles Daly catalogued and sold side-cock drillings also. These guns were actually made by Sauer & Sohn for Daly and will be marked with "Sauer & Sohn Suhl" on the barrels. Stated barrel length for the Daly guns was 28 inches and they will be very similar to Sauer's Model XXV and XXVI with gun weights from 7 to 7-3/4 pounds. The rifle barrels will be chambered for Winchesters 30-30 & 38-55. The Daly marketed side-cocker drillings will have Sauer & Sohn's manufacturing marks on the barrel flats and water table. These marks of course are Sauer & Sohn's well-known "man with staff" icon and the Sauer & Sohn inter-

twined and stylized "S". It should also be noted at this point that Sauer & Sohn actually supplied virtually all of the drillings for Charles Daly from the beginning of that company's earliest marketing efforts up until sometime well after WWI. This author has seen and handled Daly hammer drillings that dated from the latter 1880s as well as the much later Daly sidelock side-cock drilling models. Every example inspected bore the Sauer & Sohn manufacturing marks. On close examination, it is easy to see that these Daly sidelock side-cock drillings were 100 percent Sauer-built from the engraving on their frames to the matting on their ribs to the grip caps used on their buttstocks. These guns of course will not have some of the more common finishing touches as found on Sauer guns produced for Germany's domestic market, namely the interesting muzzle end barrel treatment of cross hatching between the upper and lower ribs.

It is not uncommon for the owners of the Sauer side-cocker drillings to carry a round chambered in the rifle barrel while afield in pursuit of birds during the deer season. Many owners of side-cocker drillings consider this to be a safe practice, as the tumbler/hammer of the rifle barrel is not cocked until one pushes down the sidelever to cock the tumbler of the rifle barrel. *I do not endorse this practice for the following reason.* Repeated firing of the shotgun barrels with a cartridge loaded in the rifle barrel has shown that occasionally, the shock of recoil will dislodge the bullet from the case and allow the bullet to creep forward in the case and into the forward chamber area. Through these cumulative effects of recoil, there may even exist the possibility of the bullet being driven into the bore of the rifle barrel. This of course could prove to be disastrous if the bullet were loose in the forward area of the chamber, or if the bullet had somehow managed to engage the rifling of the bore when the rear trigger was pulled and would result in a large pressure spike. In all likelihood, if such an event were to occur, the result at a minimum, would be damage to the barrel(s) and in the worst case could result in severe injury to the shooter or anyone unlucky enough to be standing nearby.

The Sauer sidelock side-cock drilling system is a unique, versatile and handy weapon for those who only want, or can only afford one firearm for all of one's hunting and shooting needs. Machine made and yet masterfully finished by hand, the inherent quality of Sauer & Sohn's sidelock side-cock drilling and its design are deserving of a closer look.

Resources: The Standard Directory of Proof Marks *by Gerhard Wirnsberger and various J.P. Sauer & Sohn & Charles Daly catalogue reprints.*
The following individuals have contributed in one form or another to make this article possible: Kirby Hoyt, Scott King, Bill Wise, and Michael Petrov.

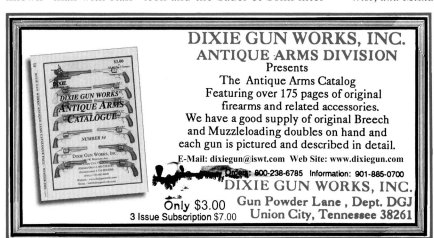

Elmer Keith

An Early And Able Advocate Of Double Rifles

by J.E. Fender

He was extremely opinionated, certainly politically incorrect by today's standards, possessed a limited formal education, and was rarely photographed without a pipe or cigar in his mouth. His refusal to see issues in any but the starkest hues of black or white with no latitude for compromise alienated a lot of people. There was no equivocation with firearms' writer Elmer Keith. You knew exactly where he stood; you either liked and defended the man as part of the "cult of the big bore"— alive and well today, or you dismissed him as a prejudiced braggart or crank. But Elmer Keith appreciated British double rifles and British large-bore cartridges, and beginning more than 50 years ago he set out to educate American hunters about the advantages, beauty, and elegance of fine double rifles. Though he has been dead for almost 20 years, it is not far-fetched at all to in fact attribute the awakening of Americans' interest in fine double rifles to Keith's extensive writings.

Although born in Missouri, Keith is associated with Montana where he grew up, and Idaho where he lived most of his adult life. He was interested in anything that would shoot—handgun, shotgun, or rifle—and from the beginning of his shooting career Keith concentrated on large-bore firearms. Keith was a son of honest toil, and supported his family by ranching and farming, as a big game guide and booking agent, and lastly as a prolific writer on the subject of firearms. Encouraged by the editor of the *American Rifleman* magazine, Chauncey Thomas, Keith published his first article, "Bullet Experience on Big Game" in the April 1925 issue of the *Rifleman*, for which he was paid the princely sum of ten dollars.

In those far away times, firearms' editors were expected to answer personally the myriad letters addressed to them in care of the magazines for which they wrote. As a youth coming of age in the late 1950s and greatly interested in firearms, I wrote to all of the firearms' editors of the "big three" sporting magazines and to the technical editors of the *American Rifleman*, as well as to John Amber, then editor of the *Gun Digest*. In those halcyon days, no matter how inane my request, I expected a personal reply as a subscriber's inalienable right. I was never disappointed, and greatly treasure a

Elmer at his desk in Salmon, Idaho.

Courtesy of *Sun Magazine*

file of letters exchanged with Amber, Keith, Jack O'Connor and Townsend Whelen.

If the reader will permit me a slight personal digression, because those writers responded to my letters, I have always believed it is my responsibility to reply as completely as possible to readers' letters forwarded to me by various editors. If an article of mine engendered questions and a reader expressed an opinion or requested further information about something I had written, the reader obviously was interested in what I had to say. Because writers like Keith took the time to respond to my queries, it naturally followed that simple courtesy required a similar response from me. Readers are perceptive critics, and it has always been a privilege to respond to their queries.

Keith purchased his first double rifle before the horrific bloodletting that was World War Two began, most probably in the early years of the Great Depression. Though it seems almost surreal to say so in the year 2003, double rifles, particularly the highest-quality British and Continental marques and calibers were totally unappreciated in the pre- and post-war 1940s and throughout the 1950s. I won't tell you what I paid for a .500/.465 Westley Richards best grade with hand-detachable locks and that great Westley Richards quality when the double rifle was offered to me, but I can tell you that I have respectfully declined offers of $30,000 for the rifle.

Elmer Keith was a gun trader, a good one, and at one time or another he owned at least a dozen double rifles. The first double rifle that was mentioned in any depth in Keith's writings was a Westley Richards .400. In the spring of 1939 he partnered with Arthur Kinnan, a brother of Marjorie Kinnan Rawlings, author of that great novel of the 1930s, *The Yearling*, to guide hunters for bear in Alaska. The .400 was not further identified, but it was most probably the .450/.400 Nitro Express 3-inch Jeffery-designed cartridge, and Keith employed it as his guide's rifle. He reported having used the .400 Jeffery "a good bit," and considered the cartridge in a double rifle "a wonderful close range stopper on any game on this [North American] continent." When and how Keith acquired this rifle will probably never be known, but I suspect that,

Photography by David Trevallion unless otherwise noted.

given the times, Keith did not pay a great deal of money in relative terms for it, though of course the cost would have been very dear for him.

In *Elmer Keith's Big Game Hunting*, first published in 1948, and which summarized his experiences over 30-plus years of hunting and guiding, Keith argued his case for the practicality of double rifles in chapter 4, "Timber and All-Around Rifles":

"In a fine double-barrel hammerless ejector rifle, we have to my notion one of the nicest, if not the nicest, of all timber rifles. It balances about like your favorite shotgun, yet has more weight for steadiness, low easily defined open sights that swing easily onto the mark, and the fastest of all safeties. Further, the double rifle is closed tighter against rain, snow, sleet or falling pine and fir needles than any type of repeating rifle. You have two shots, instantly available without working any pump action, lever action or bolt, or the rattling jar of an autoloader."

We could add to the list our appreciation of the double rifle's aesthetic qualities, but Keith certainly captured the admirable qualities of the double rifle quite well.

Elmer Keith visited Trevallion's Indiana workshop on his way to accept the first American Handgunner of the Year Award.

He subsequently wrote that a good bolt action large-bore rifle would cost $300, while a good double rifle might cost twice that.

Any firearms' enthusiast knowledgeable of the Great Depression years prior to World War Two and the lean years following will confirm there was very little interest in double rifles. Double rifles were considered passé; few people were purchasing them. In the period 1935–1955, a fine double rifle, new or used, from a highest-quality British or Continental maker could often be had for less than one thousand dollars. Of course, inflation has taken its toll of our currency, and it takes almost ten thousand of today's dollars to purchase what one thousand dollars could purchase in 1950.

Interestingly, though, a sturdy, well-kept Continental-built double rifle chambered for a large-bore British caliber, such as the Krieghoff, Heym, or Chapuis can be purchased today for something like $8,500 on average. These utilitarian doubles do not have the cachet of the British "best" makers, but having shot and hunted with the

G A GUNS & AMMO MAGAZINE • ELMER KEITH SHOOTING EDITOR | SALMON, IDAHO

March 11th-67

Dear David:

I have my orders to go back to W'sh D.C. and attend the NRA Convention for the magazine. Dates are March 31st through 6th pri; so will probably be going back a day ahead of time. Have put my 500-3" Charles Boswrll in an old shotgun case and will bring along and either stay over aday in Chi or try get Joe to meet me at the air port and get the 500 from me to deliver to you for the new stock.

It has a perfectly good stock now but too much cast off that I dont need at all and thin comb and no cheek piece. As its in perfect shape inside and shoots wonderful both barrels right on center at 50 yards is well worth restocking. I also have comp/onkents enough for 600 rounds and also over 100 rounds Kyncoh loads as well. Dont need any cast off and think a stock on very similiar lines to the one you had on the 600 would be fine. Will check dimensions but think about 14½ to front trigger with comb of 1 5/8 but not over 2¼" heel drop about right. Will try get another of those big rounded corner sold pads that Pachmayr sent to C H in Enid for it. It has a very deep butt plate which is well with the 500 loads and is pleasant to shoot, now but will be a lot more so when you get one of your good stocks on it and think tha blank you saved for me will do the job nicely. Like to have a good photo of the gun with old stock and then with the new one so can write it up for my column . If you have to make new foreend to match the stock then either like present one which is sound and good or a small thin beavertail that just comes around the barrels and is not wide and bulky like the old Parker shotgun beavertails. Think grip should be around 5¼" in circumferance and you can give me a more curved and better pistol grip than one on the rifle now. Down pitch should be 1½ to not over 2". Its a bloody good rifle and will be better with one of your fine handles on it. George Neary killed six elephant and a lot of buff with it in Tanganyika. Tanzania now.

May try and stay over night with Joe on way back and if so hope you can run out and pick up the gun or he can deliver later. All the best to you and your good lady and hope to see you ere too long.

Sincerely,
Keith

Elmer

BEND 1⅝X2¼.
LENGTH 14½
CHST - 0°
PITCH 2"

TRUNK CASE FOR THIS RIFLE?

GUNS & AMMO HOME OFFICE: 5959 HOLLYWOOD BLVD., LOS ANGELES 28, CALIF.

Letter written by Elmer Keith to David Trevallion in which Keith describes the dimensions he wants David to incorporate into the new stock of Keith's .500 Boswell. Keith clearly knew what he wanted for the new stock's dimensions. The hand-scribed notations in the lower left corner are David's notes.

Krieghoff and Chapuis extensively, I can truthfully represent they are fully as capable of faithfully discharging the duties of the double rifle as their more prestigious British cousins.

Keith was able to hunt twice in Africa. He had been invited by John Lawrence, one of the top professional hunters in Kenya, to an expenses paid safari, provided Keith paid his way to Kenya. In November of 1957, Keith pitched up in Nairobi with a best-quality Westley Richards chambered in the Westley Richards-developed .476 Nitro-Express cartridge, and a .333 OKH bolt gun built on a Mauser action. The .333 OKH was developed by Keith and two associates, C.M. O'Neil and Donald Hopkins; the cartridge was the venerable .30-06 case given a new shoulder angle and necked up to accept bullets designed for the .333 Jeffery. The designer's intent was to duplicate the ballistics of the .333 Jeffery, and the cartridge met that goal. In a

A montage of photographs—from the left, Elmer Keith in David Trevallion's Chicago, Illinois, shop. Keith is holding the original buttstock of the .500 Boswell. Even in Chicago, Keith was not without his trademark .44 magnum Smith and Wesson handgun!

Top photograph, a much younger David holding the .500 Boswell with its original stock while Keith holds the stock blank he had selected; right photograph shows Keith critically examining the blank. Bottom photograph shows Keith standing between David and Joe Merrill, a mutual friend of David's and Keith's. The inscription beneath this photograph indicates that David had paid $86 for the stock blank a year earlier.

PATTERN, PISTOL GRIP FOR E. KEITH. IDAHO.

.500 Boswell D/RIFLE.
SR No 17109

CHEEK PIECE. JP PAT.
SILVER OVAL.
SLING SWIVEL EYE.
SIDE PANELS
DROP POINTS

CHEQUERED PANEL

TANG

DIAM.

LENGTH OF 'POLL'
WITH PAD.
RED R.PAD.

ELMER KEITHS
THUMB PRINT (LEFT HAND)
MARCH 1967. CHICAGO.

STEEL CAP

(TRAP DOOR).

Full-scale drawing of the dimensions David Trevallion intended to craft into the buttstock he would create for Elmer Keith. Such painstaking detail in planning prior to execution is the hallmark of a master stockmaker! Left: Trevallion carving cheekpiece on the .500 Boswell stock for Elmer Keith.
Photo by Darlene Trevallion

month and a half with John Lawrence, Keith took the traditional big five animals, including leopard, with the .476, and plains game such as sable, roan, eland and kudu with the .338 OKH.

Keith was invited to hunt elephant in Kenya in the latter half of 1969 as the guest of a well-to-do Californian, Truman

Fowler. He was also invited to accompany a party made up of shooters from the Petersen Publishing Company, to Uganda and Tanzania, and hunted with them for ten days before rendezvousing with Fowler in Kenya. For this lengthy safari Keith elected to take only one rifle, a Charles Boswell boxlock chambered for the .500 Nitro-Express 3 inch, the favorite cartridge of the legendary John A. Hunter. From the serial number, 17109, and the 126 Strand address in the West End of London, this double was probably built between 1906 and 1910, though the serial number range indicates the double rifle was sold from the factory in 1913. Keith obtained this double rifle from a George Neary, "who had killed six elephant and a good many buffalo with the rifle." I have been frustrated in my attempts to learn more about George Neary, but believe that he was an American

GUNS & AMMO MAGAZINE • ELMER KEITH SHOOTING EDITOR | SALMON, IDAHO

June 19th-68

Dear David:

    Took the Boswell out to the range and fired a couple rounds at 50 yards, I belive it was and shot exactly same as before you put that fine stock on it-one bullet just underthe other and perfect. This stock fits like a dream and is ever so much better than the old one.
    I been waiting thinking you would send me a picture of the job so I could put another paragraph or two on your work in my column as no photographer here that can do good gun photos. It's a splendid job but am having Iver Henriksen put a stonger spring in that safety as moves forward too easy now. Also have him make and fit a dourdough blade front sight and hood for it as well.
    Come see us when ever you get out this way and am sure Darlene is right and if you live a shory time here in the Northwest you would never again be happy any place else and they are not so damn anti-gun crazy here. This Boswell has less recoil than any big double I own, must be partly the fine straight stock as is pleasant to shoot off a bench rest even. I picked up a best Westley Richards 577 with extra locks and in pretty fair shape but has a no cheek rest stock but sound and of all things cast-in for a south paw but the bend comes rigyt at the pistol grip so dont seem to bother me and sights line up good when it comes up. 13 lb four ounces.Been used a good bit and still very good and shoots well. Freind thinking of taking me to Africa next year and will take the Boswell or this 577 as we will be after elephant and big buff only.
    Glad the hand is now O.K. I once ran a big screw driver ough my left hand when it slipped and know what it is
    Give Bob Pflaumer and the Merrills my best when you see will be looking for you folks out this way in Aug. me a 5X 7 print of best photo you took of the Boswell so ou some more publicity on it in my column.

                                    Sincerely,
                                    Keith

                                    Elmer

GUNS & AMMO HOME OFFICE: 5959 HOLLYWOOD BLVD., LOS ANGELES 28, CALIF.

ELMER WITH PARKER 12ga DB A1SP.
- MY OFFICE "HURLINGHAM FARM" INDIANA.
DAY RAMER RECIVED THE 1ST HANDGUNNER OF
THE YEAR" AWARD. FROM LEE JURAS.

A letter written by Elmer Keith to David Trevallion summarizing the results and accuracy of Keith's .500 Boswell after David had restocked this double rifle. This letter is a good example of Keith's writing—and demonstrates why his writing required a lot of editing before being printed—about which he complained frequently! Keith is holding a Parker A1 Special shotgun that David had just stocked.

who hunted Africa frequently. However, the quote above is all that Keith ever said about the source of the .500 Boswell.

There was only one thing wrong with the .500 Boswell when Keith acquired it and a supply of ammunition in 1965 or 1966—the stock did not fit him. But Keith knew of an exceptional "English gun stocker" and in a March 11, 1967, letter he described the buttstock's problems to Purdey-

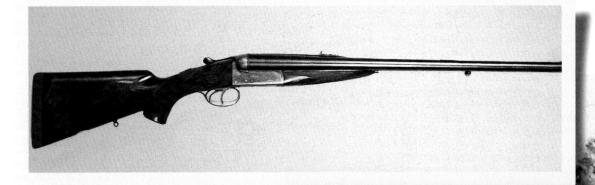

The .500 Boswell double rifle stocked by David Trevallion to Elmer Keith's specifications.
A photograph of Elmer, showing the largest elephant he killed with his .500 Boswell—restocked by David Trevallion.
And, at far right, a photograph of Keith trying the double rifle's fit after taking delivery.

trained stockmaker David Trevallion, whose gun shop was then located in Chicago. "It has a perfectly good stock now but too much cast off that I don't need at all and thin comb and no cheek piece." As you can see in the accompanying letter, Keith certainly knew the stock dimensions he wanted. Keith subsequently visited David's gun shop to drop off the Boswell and look over stock blanks David had available, selecting a magnificent piece of French walnut.

David delivered the restocked .500 Boswell in early November 1967, on the date promised, exactly to Keith's specifications, after devoting 33 hours of labor in shaping, inletting, checkering, fitting a recoil pad supplied by Pachmayr Guns, balancing the weight of the new buttstock to the weight of the original stock, and applying the stock finish. David also invested three hours in refinishing the forend to match the finish of the new buttstock. By the time various administrative chores such as corresponding with Keith were accomplished, David had expended well over a week's work in the .500 Boswell, but the Charles Boswell double rifle weighed the exact same 12 and 1/4 pounds it weighed when it arrived in David's shop.

Keith may not have known the opportunities for a lengthy African sojourn would arise when he commissioned the work in 1967, and he was also recovering from a massive coronary. But when Truman Fowler's invitation to hunt for big elephant in 1969 came, as well as the subsequent opportunity to join the Petersen Publishing Company safari, Elmer Keith had a double rifle that fitted him perfectly. Keith spent ten days in late September with the Petersen group in Uganda and Tanzania, and employed the .500 Boswell to kill two Cape buffalo, the first at a paced 140 yards from Keith's sitting posi-

tion. Keith also killed a large hippopotamus with the Boswell.

Keith rendezvoused with Fowler in Nairobi and put in thirty days hunting in a large concession on the Galana River, solely for elephant. Keith had his .500 Boswell, of course, and Fowler had fetched along a .577 Nitro-Express Charles Lancaster double rifle weighing 15 pounds that Keith had sold him. Keith killed three elephant bulls with his Boswell and Fowler killed one. You won't find the story about Keith's last African hunt in the book, *Safari*, because that book was published in 1968 and was actually an example of "vanity press" privately published by Fowler. Though Keith was listed as the

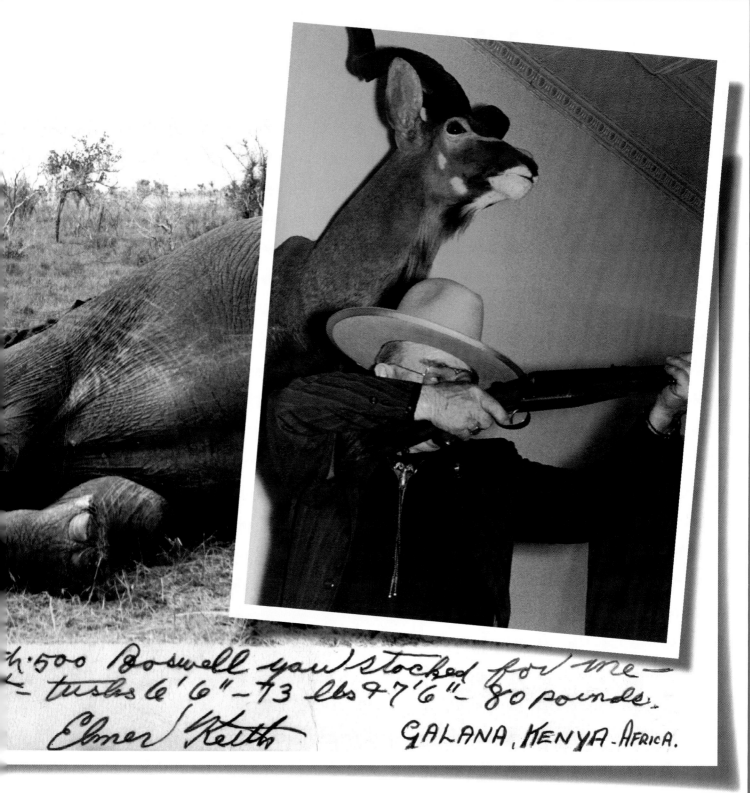

h.500 Boswell yau stocked for me — — tusks 6'6" — 73 lbs & 7'6" — 80 pounds.

Elmer Keith

GALANA, KENYA - AFRICA.

author, a good portion of the material was furnished by Fowler. You can read about Keith's employment of his double rifles during two African hunts in *Keith: An Autobiography*, published in 1974 and *Hell, I Was There!* published in 1979. There is a great deal of repetition in these two books, but they are not different titles for the same book.

Ex-cowpuncher Elmer Keith may seem an unlikely voice in educating American hunters to the advantages of the well-built double rifle, and certainly there were other writers who wrote of the double rifles' advantages; but he spoke out early and he spoke out often. I for one am very glad that he did. And I'm also very glad that Keith would entrust the restocking of his .500 Boswell to no one but David Trevallion. My warmest thanks to David for graciously sharing his voluminous file of correspondence with Elmer Keith and photographs of Keith and his guns with the readers of the *Double Gun Journal*.

Editor's Note: In the 40-plus years since he sold his first article to Boys' Life *magazine, Jim Fender has published over 3,000 articles in every outdoors and sporting magazine of any consequence. He is the author of the* Geoffrey Frost Saga, *nautical fiction published by the University Press of New England that examines the American Revolution through the eyes of a privateer captain.*

Woodcock Shooting
Etching by A. Lassell Ripley
Courtesy of The Sporting Gallery & Bookshop, Pennington, NJ

The Perfect Gift For Double Gun Journal Subscribers!

If you haven't already purchased *The Double Gun Journal Index & Reader, Volume I*, you should do so soon. Supplies are diminishing and we do not plan to reprint once they are sold out. See our advertisement on page 81 of this issue, at right. To order: use this form or call 800-447-1658.

If you have already purchased Volume I and are awaiting the publication of *The Double Gun Journal Index & Reader, Volume II*, you will be happy to know that we plan publication later next year. We will send you advanced notice so you may reserve your copy.

The Double Gun Journal Index & Reader, Volume I

Slipcases and The DGJ Index & Reader are pictured on page 81 of this issue, at right.

*A 250 page full-color leather bound hardcover book, containing an Index which provides research access to every name and subject discussed/mentioned throughout our first 7 years **plus** 150 pages, 40 new articles and century-old hunting and safari stories written by those who were there. For a complete list of contents please see below, or just give us a call @ 800-447-1658*

LIST OF CONTENTS

To order, please see the reverse side of this card – or just call us @ 800-447-1658 or 231-536-7439
To fax your order: 231-536-7450

The Double Gun Journal
Subscription & Gift Order Form

☐ Start my subscription/gift subscription to the *Journal* @ **$39⁹⁵**/year. (22% off the $52 cover price.)

☐ As a current subscriber I would like to renew my subscription and/or send:

✱ ____ gift subscriptions/gift renewals @ **$37** each. ☐ Send a Gift card with my greetings (enclosed).

▶ SUBSCRIBERS SHOULD RECEIVE THEIR COPIES PRIOR TO NEWSSTANDS & BOOKSTORES. ◀

Gift No. 1 To:
Name _____
Address _____
_____
City _____
State/Country _____ Zip _____

Gift No. 2 To:
Name _____
Address _____
_____
City _____
State/Country _____ Zip _____

Gift No. 3 To: (You get 1 free year.)
Name _____
Address _____
_____
City _____
State/Country _____ Zip _____

FREE ▶ Give 3 subscriptions or gift renewals and we'll extend your subscription 1 year Free. ◀ FREE
✱ SORRY, THE THREE (3) GIFTS & RENEWALS (FREE OFFER) MAY NOT INCLUDE YOUR OWN SUBSCRIPTION

Available Back Issues– As long as supplies last – there are no plans to reprint these volumes:

☐ VOLUME III - 1992, Issues 1-4 .... $135.00
Ship these only: ☐ Issue 1 ☐ Issue 2 ☐ Issue 3 ☐ Issue 4 @ $45 ea.

☐ VOLUME IV - 1993, Issues 1-4 .... $120.00
Ship these only: ☐ Issue 1 ☐ Issue 2 ☐ Issue 3 ☐ Issue 4 @ $40 ea.

☐ VOLUME V - 1994, Issues 1-4 .... $100.00
Ship these only: ☐ Issue 1 ☐ Issue 2 ☐ Issue 3 ☐ Issue 4 @ $35 ea.

☐ VOLUME VI - 1995, Issues 1-4 .... $100.00
Ship these only: ☐ Issue 1 ☐ Issue 2 ☐ Issue 3 ☐ Issue 4 @ $35 ea.

☐ VOLUME VII - 1996, Issues 1-4 .... $90.00
Ship these only: ☐ Issue 1 ☐ Issue 2 ☐ Issue 3 ☐ Issue 4 @ $30 ea.

☐ VOLUME VIII - 1997, Issues 1 & 2 ..... $50.00
Ship these @ $35 ea.: ☐ Issue 1 ☐ Issue 2 (Issues 3 & 4 - CALL US)

☐ VOLUME IX - 1998, Issues 1-4 .... $80.00
Ship these only: ☐ Issue 1 ☐ Issue 2 ☐ Issue 3 ☐ Issue 4 @ $30 ea.

☐ VOLUME X - 1999, Issues 1-4 .... $70.00
Ship these only: ☐ Issue 1 ☐ Issue 2 ☐ Issue 3 ☐ Issue 4 @ $25 ea.

☐ VOLUME XI - 2000, Issues 1-4 .... $60.00
Ship these only: ☐ Issue 1 ☐ Issue 2 ☐ Issue 3 ☐ Issue 4 @ $20 ea.

☐ VOLUME XII - 2001, Issues 1-4 .... $50.00
Ship these only: ☐ Issue 1 ☐ Issue 2 ☐ Issue 3 ☐ Issue 4 @ $15 ea.

☐ VOLUME XIII - 2002, Issues 1-4 .... $50.00
Ship these only: ☐ Issue 1 ☐ Issue 2 ☐ Issue 3 ☐ Issue 4 @ $15 ea.

Sporting Gifts You Will Not Find <u>Anywhere</u> Else.

Leather Slipcases

☐ Ship Slipcase(s) for Volumes: I, II, III, IV, V, VI, VII, VIII, IX, X, XI, XII, XIII, XIV @ $16⁷⁵ each.
All gold stamped slipcases are individualized – please circle the slipcases you need – slipcases are pictured at right.

☐ **The Double Gun Journal Index & Reader** @ $49⁹⁵ppd is pictured at right. *A 250 page full-color leather bound hardcover book, containing an Index which provides research access to every name and subject discussed/mentioned throughout our first 7 years **plus** 150 pages, 40 new articles and century-old hunting and safari stories written by those who were there. For a complete List Of Contents please refer to overleaf – or just give us a call @ 800-447-1658.*

☐ *Original* **Parker** *Gus Peret* **Posters** - *Only a few of these remain* - see page 136, Summer 2003.
Ship ____ 4/C ____ B/W version(s) @ $65 each (both for $115 ppd.) 12 3/4" x 16 1/2"

☐ **English Gun Catalogues** - *see page 136, Summer 2003.*
Westley Richards, $28 • James Woodward, $14 • Chambers, $8
Buy both @ $40 ppd – Please encircle your choice(s)

☐ **Shooting Scenes** - by *A.L. Ripley; 6 different scenes, 14 cards & envelopes. Send* ____ *sets @ $17 ea., $30/two*

☐ **A. L. Ripley Limited Edition Lithographs**
"Woodcock Shooting"- $125ppd
"Hunting For Pheasant" - $55ppd.

Collect both prints in matching Limited Edition numbers all for $155ppd. *For more information about these prints see our ad on page 114 of Summer 2003.*

In A Hurry? Please Call Or Fax And We Can Expedite Your Order To Arrive By That Special Day!
We accept VISA, MC, AMEX, MO or Check in U.S. FUNDS

Charge my: ☐ Visa ☐ MC ☐ AMEX   Credit Card Acct. No. _____ Exp. _____

MAIL, TELEPHONE OR FAX – VISA/MC/AMEX WILL EXPEDITE YOUR ORDER – TYPE OR PRINT CLEARLY PLEASE – GIFT CARDS AVAILABLE AT NO CHARGE

SHIP MY
SUBSCRIPTION TO: _____
_____

800-447-1658 (Orders Only)
231-536-7439 (All Questions)
Fax 231-536-7450 (24 Hr. Service)
AUTUMN 2003

The Double Gun Journal • P.O. Box 550 • East Jordan, MI 49727 U.S.A.

SHIPPING: All U.S. Orders Shipped Postpaid to Contiguous 48 States. **EXPEDITED DELIVERY:** Priority mail insured to USA add $24/year to regular rate. Overseas addresses please call us @ 231-536-7439. Subscriptions to Canada add $10 Surface Mail. **ALL OTHER COUNTRIES:** Add $12 per Yearly Subscription, $7/Slipcase, $23/*D.G.J. Index & Reader*, $12/Back-Issue Set, $6/Individual Back Issue, all via Surface Mail, Airmail by request. English Gun Catalogue Reprints & Note Cards add $6 per item via Airmail. All U.S. Funds. Visa//MC/AMEX will expedite your order.

Take Your Yield To The Field

Imagine that. An investment that can actually increase in value while you use it. Like a fine wine, your Merkel shotgun improves with age—both on the bottom line and on that balance sheet we call "enlightenment". Whether your preference is a side-by-side or over-and-under, box-lock or sidelock, every Merkel shotgun is a joy to handle and a pleasure to behold. Visit your Merkel dealer today for the investment of a lifetime that lasts a lifetime. For a full-color catalog visit our web site at www.gsifirearms.com or send a written request to the address below.

Me Bonnie MacDougall

*Written and Photographed
by William W. Headrick*

It was the late 1980s, and though Charlie and I were sadly destined never to meet, we had become real phone pals over the preceding couple of years. Exactly what precipitated his first call to the Headrick digs now escapes me, but somehow he had come by the notion that Pop and yours truly were primarily pass shooters and appreciated double guns with seriously tall reach. As it turned out, our chats usually ended up revolving around Charlie's near consuming fascination with and exhaustive knowledge of tight patterning classic American fowlers.

His files were apparently chock-full of articles and sundry bits and pieces of gleaned esoterica concerning Super Foxes, Long Range Smiths, Magnum Ithacas, Duck-designated Winchesters, and the various over-bored Remington models. In addition, he had corresponded with about every legitimately published gun crank and self-proclaimed arms authority of the day who professed sharing his penchant for such high-performance smoothbores. And, off the top of his head, my chum was capable of quoting more than most of us—including the author—would ever care to know regarding the nominal dimensions inherent to most domestic makers' barrel interiors.

Fortunately, Charlie's more generalized expertise concerning golden-age side by sides was adequate enough to keep him out of deep trouble in that sector of the marketplace. By his own admission, however, he confessed to being a real sucker for just about any scatterpiece which had potential for placing most of its shot charge in pretty much the same place at well-downrange yardages. Although principally hooked on long-chambered 12s and big 10s, it was essentially that same,

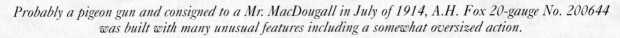

pervasive, and overriding addiction which necessitated his acquisition of the here-featured twenty-gauge Fox.

Forced into early retirement by an insidious and ever worsening health disability, Charlie spent a portion of most days combing his neck of the woods for two-barreled candidates deemed worthy of extensive pattern testing and having their innards probed with a formidable array of tools, gauges, and gadgetry. No longer able to cope with the associated rigors of full-fledged waterfowling, my friend's smoothbore shoulderings were basically limited to various backyard ballistic investigations and several temperate afternoons per season bucket-perched on a favorite dove pass. The latter was no doubt responsible for piquing, at least in part, his immediate interest in the subject double.

Whether Charlie's discovery of the pictured Fox had occurred at a gun show, flea-type market, or in one of the sporting goods shops he frequented on a regular basis, I cannot now recall. But by its obviously tight muzzle constrictions, lengthy tubes, considerable heft for a small bore, undeniably dynamic handling characteristics, lack of embellishment, and absent safety, his initial assessment of the arm was likely right on the mark—a pigeon gun, as unusual as that might be for a twenty gauge.

Thankfully, it all proved sufficiently intriguing for him to make the deal and head for the patterning plates. Within a week, that lovely and never to be forgotten Virginia drawl greeted my response to the phone's evening ring.

Following the usual and customary exchange of pleasantries, Charlie cut right to the chase regarding his most

*Probably a pigeon gun and consigned to a Mr. MacDougall in July of 1914, A.H. Fox 20-gauge No. 200644
was built with many unusual features including a somewhat oversized action.*

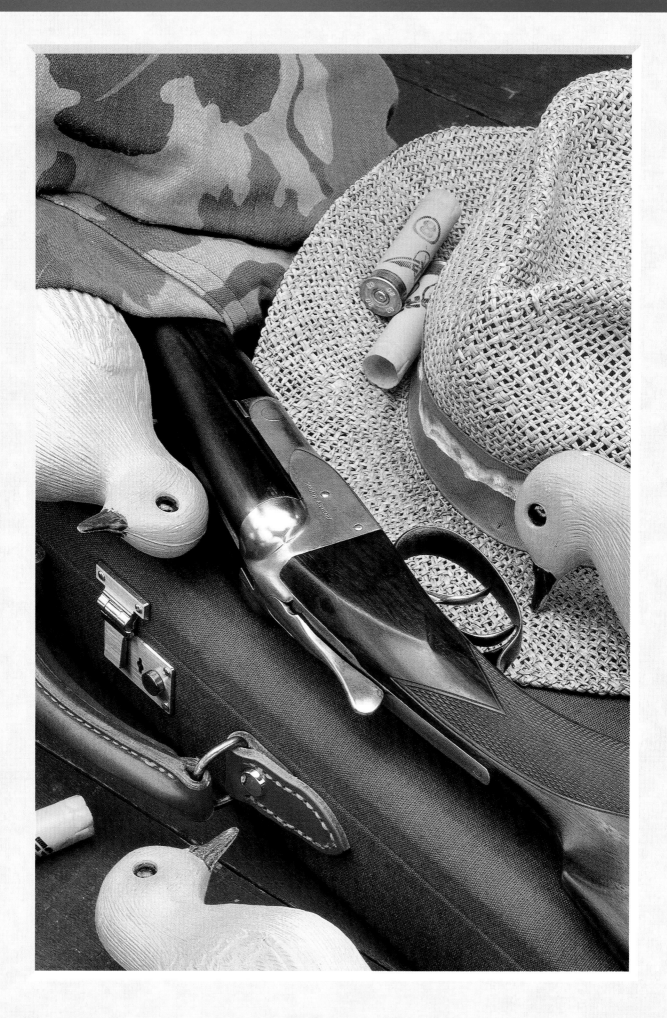

Although rather standard factory stampings, a lot of Fox guns from this period are not marked with an indication of gauge. The steel disc in the underside of the maker's so-called snap-on forearm serves only as an anchoring reinforcement for those arms ejector optioned.

Below: Company advertising described the shown forearm latching with "...a new Fox spiral spring creation, and acts as one of the greatest compensating devices ever placed on any gun." Flamboyant but true. Originally meant for all gauges of the maker's entry-level Sterlingworth, the early graded and ejector-equipped small bores utilized the same mechanism.

recent acquisition. An ejector-equipped A Grade without engraving, the stout twenty remained as tight and dead-on-face as the day it was completed—probably during the early teens by its serial number and snap-on forearm latching. The gun's bores were brilliant, the top lever well right of center, and an original buttplate capped-off what appeared to be dense, structurally sound, and uncut lumber. My chum conceded, however, that the piece exhibited a number of what he referred to as minor cosmetic irregularities. None of which, fortunately, had been offensive enough to dissuade him from fetching it homeward.

Apparently some industrious soul with a lot of time on his hands and an ample supply of fine steel wool had removed virtually every trace of case color from the Fox's action exterior and top lever. Likely it was the same well-intentioned, though misguided, restoration artist who managed to generally botch a

reblue job on the twenty's barrels. And at least a coat or two of less than totally transparent mystery finish had been generously brushed over the gun's woodwork. Stock and forearm alike. Dirt, grime, checkering, and all. Other than that...

I sensed what was coming and sure enough it did. Matters of frivolity duly reported and rather hurriedly dispensed with, Charlie launched into what he deemed to be the real meat and potato issues regarding the Fox: how it shot and the physics responsible for it doing so.

Already in particularly high form and warming to the subject as he went, my chum delivered a veritable dissertation containing, amongst much other, a detailed, exacting, and tediously incremental analysis of the twenty's tube interiors from stem to stern. All, of course, was expressed in terms requiring a minimum of three-decimal-place precision. In addition, he spewed

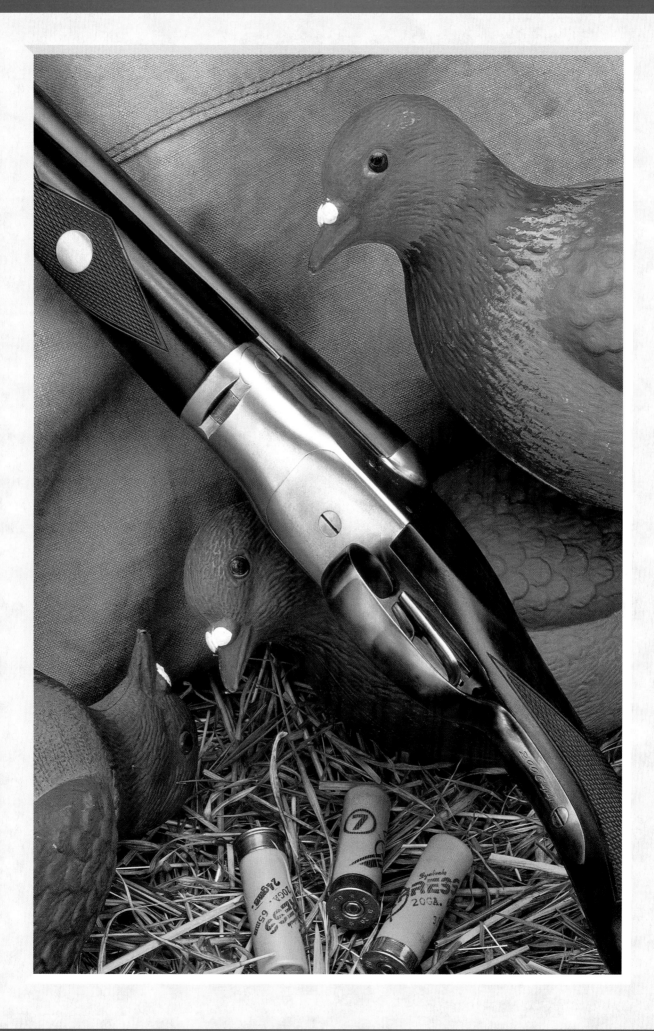

forth a seemingly endless stream of figures concerning yardages, circle diameters, impact points, pattern distributions, pellet counts, and payload percentages.

In due time, however, and in his now delightfully brief and refreshingly technical-free summation, Charlie proclaimed this particular example of "The Finest Gun in the World" to shoot like the proverbial house afire. In fact, he stated unequivocally that the subject twenty patterned consistently tighter and more evenly than any scatterpiece of any gauge he had thus far tested using No. 6s, 7½s, 8s, and 9s. Exactly why this set of barrels performed so splendidly

Such knowledge, coupled with an awareness of the subject gun's beefier-than-usual action and barrel-breech regions, had prompted him to at least perform his testing procedures using low-base standard velocity, and over-the-counter-purchased ammunition. He further declared having no compunctions toward feeding the hefty Fox a steady diet of the same stuff if necessary.

But the big twenty's lack of a safety made him more than a little uneasy, and although the gun had never doubled, the trigger pulls were far lighter than he would likely ever become accustomed to. In truth, on several or so occasions

The McIntosh-prescribed butt extension also accommodates his suggested change in down-pitch; and like the rear of 200644's stock, was housed-out in order to preserve the gun's original weight, balance, and splendid dynamics. Once worn or polished bright, Fox actions forged and machined from the company's celebrated "Chromox" steel tend to stay that way indefinitely.

remained a ponderable warranting his continued investigation—especially in light of then current and accepted wisdom which predicted it simply should not have.

Grossly overchoked and somewhat underbored, the tubes retained their original short chambers, steeply angled forcing cones, and the maker's all but four inches of slowly tapered squeeze. An additional and goodly portion of parallel had been provided forward of both excessive constrictions, and all therein was flawlessly honed and polished to a mirrorlike fare-thee-well by some unknown Fox-employed wizard.

Now nearly a decade and a half ago, imported cartridges ideally suited to the short chamber dimensions of vintage doubles were not to be had in Charlie's nor most folks' neighborhoods. Be that as it may, my pal was already well acquainted with the but slight pressure increases generated by thin plastic shot-shell cases exhibiting only a quarter-inch of extra length.

and during the relatively excitement-free atmosphere of shooting at a whitewashed plate of steel, the Fox had seemingly touched itself off a bit before my pal was quite ready to take the shot. He could just imagine how events might unfold in the field with birds on the wing and his adrenaline pump revving at an increased rate. Besides, despite the gun shooting precisely to the point of aim, it really did not fit him all that well. And…

The pictured Fox, No. 200644, was brown truck delivered to the Headrick digs late that same week. Prior to its arrival, a couple of phone chats with the authorized Savage-Stevens-Fox historian in those days, Mr. Roe S. Clark, confirmed the twenty's basic righteousness as per the arm's thankfully remaining and on file production record. Occasionally encountered among the existing and approximately 190,000 shop cards, No. 200644's was one of those which raised as many or more ques-

Observe how narrow the gun's top rib has become after 30 inches of taper. Unfortunately, the original ivory front bead needed replacing after encountering a steel fence post. Compare the elegant shaping and profiling of 200644's trigger spoons and blades to those usually encountered on Foxes of this catalogued price range.

tions than it answered—especially with the gun unwrapped, assembled, in hand, and under eye.

Based on the quarter century of Fox exposure already under my belt and notwithstanding the gun's lack of engraving, absent safety, and select quality wood, it was clear that before me was no run-of-the-mill and garden variety AE Grade. Nor, without a real imagination stretching, could the arm have been built solely on the basis of its production-card-provided information which I had carefully recorded during Roe Clark's long-distance revelations.

A more likely scenario continues to suggest that Mr. MacDougall—the gun's original consignee of record—or someone acting on his behalf, either worked at Fox during the middle months of 1914 or, at minimum, was well acquainted with an individual who did. Whatever those now long ago and speculative circumstances, No. 200644's birthing had surely been, in industry parlance, an inside job.

Though shop card specified and water table stamped as an ejector A Grade, a note on the gun's production record indicates there was to be "no engraving on action or barrels." It would seem such penned instructions were not to be taken lightly, as the pictured arm lingered in the company's embellishment department only long enough for "Ansley H. Fox" to be incised on its frame sides and the serial number cut into the triggerguard tang. Other than that, not a line or accent or squiggle appears anywhere on 200644's metalwork.

Mr. MacDougall's bespoken stock particulars were then

barely outside the maker's catalogue-prescribed parameters for trap-configured arms, and it was not all that uncommon for the era's live-bird guns to exhibit comb and heel drops commensurate with popular field dimensions. In 1914 and despite an ever waning participation in competitive pigeon shooting, the sport still survived—albeit on a somewhat more clandestine and politically correct basis—with regularly held events continuing to occur but a short drive's distance from Fox's Philadelphia factory.

Well prior to 200644's building, independent safeties had become the option of choice for those involved in the ever more popular game of breaking clay discs, and orders for genuine live-bird guns without some form or variation of the device dwindled to all but none by the mid teens. Even during the company's earliest years of production, relatively few 12-bore Foxes were built without a safety, and the author has yet to hear of another twenty so configured.

Full and full hardly begins to describe the featured arm's muzzle constrictions or the devastatingly dense and identical patterns generated by its tightly squeezed tubes. Brownell's best-quality choke gauge—a combination 12-, 16-, and 20-bore instrument—fails by a little going in one side and does not come close to entering the other.

Such diameter differences are usually the result of some master barrel-smith's fine tuning and tweaking in order to achieve the desired payload percentages. As often as not, these laboriously crafted guns—seldom Sterlingworths, AE,

or BE Grades—are discovered to have pattern testing results written on the backs of their shop cards. But 200644's card shows only a rubber stamping of the serial number and bit of illegible scribbling which might possibly include a company employee's initials.

Admonishing the Fox artisans that the pictured arm "must be exactly as ordered," 200644's production record lacked a couple of important details at the project's very onset. A close inspection of the document reveals the big twenty's intended weight to have been eventually penciled in and by a different hand than that of the original office force

AE Grade, the deletion is here conspicuous. Particularly so when, upon Charlie's urging, it was determined the front trigger set things in motion at a bit over three pounds, the back one requiring just a tad more pressure. My old bro, Michael McIntosh, claims they are in all respects as fine a pair of triggers as he has ever encountered on any double of any make from any country at any price. Enough said.

Alerting the shop force with a note to "select nice stock" was obviously sufficient for the good Mr. MacDougall to take delivery of a gun wooded and style enhanced at least a couple quality tiers above that normally associated with AE-

All but the lightest Fox offered, these No. 3 weight tubes were selected for their particularly robust breeches. And this small bore's top rib is as wide and heavy at the rear as observed on any of the maker's 20-gauge guns.

scribe. And a yet later entry suggests an even greater heft as more accurately describing the completed gun—all evidence of a work in progress, the evolutionary process overseen and directed by an on-site or at least often present individual.

Foundationed on a somewhat oversized action, the subject arm tips the scales to within a couple ounces of the heaviest twenties offered in the *1914 Fox Gets The Game* catalogue. Barreled with a pair of the maker's relatively light though robustly breeched tubes, 200644's considerable heft is decidedly between the hands and balances exactly on the hinge pin's leading edge. Both swamped and extremely tapered, the top rib of MacDougall's creation is unique among those guns touted to be "The Finest in the World."

Never included on its work order record was mention of 200644's trigger pull weights. The shop cards of Fox's low-end guns seldom list this specification, but considering the special-order nature and probable intended use of the pictured

level Foxes. The lumber—itself French, English, or Circassian thinshell—is more akin to that reserved for use on the maker's CE- or XE-strata arms, and 200644's butt-stock and forearm are both fashioned from the same richly colored and densely figured blank. Although the checkering pattern is standard for an AE Grade of 1914, the lines per inch, general execution, ebony inlaid forearm tip, and silver stock shield are features well beyond that routinely encountered on the company's next to the bottom offering.

Not revealed by 200644's production record is that MacDougall was apparently left-handed. The gun's stock is significantly cast for contact with what most of us characterize as the "off" shoulder and cheek. And when it came my way, the pitch of the triggers further verified the arm to have been built for a southpaw.

Oddly enough, the vagaries, mysteries, and downright voodoo associated with gun fit aside, 200644 came up, shouldered,

and swung as if I had been the one who placed the order at Fox rather than MacDougall. Whoever he was. By some strange and quirky coincidence, a combination of the stock's ample drop and backwards cast in conjunction with my own physique had me looking dead center and over the top of the rib. If anything...perhaps...just a little too much of the latter. Luckily,

scratch, and the use of a comfy bed in order for him to negotiate a couple hundred miles of twisted, hilly, and two-lane roads. But when he received word that my twenty-gauge Fox pigeon gun had just arrived, his Blazer was in the Headrick driveway before dark.

The bro, quickly becoming a seer of sorts regarding such matters, peered over an upraised thumb at yours truly's 6-foot 3-inch frame and yard-long sleeves, wet a forefinger to test the breeze, mumbled something about hocus and pocus, fiddled with his pipe, and jotted a few numbers on a scrap of paper.

Soon enough, a smithy well known to him had 200644 on the bench, the action stripped and cleaned, the triggers bent around for a right-hander, and the wood refinished. As per Mike's prescription, the down-pitch was slightly altered and the length of pull extended almost an inch. Interestingly, the required chunk of thinshell came from a Purdey which had passed through the chap's shop in need of a pad.

Upon her return I was hopelessly smitten, and she has been my true love and soul mate afield for the better part of a dozen years now. MacDougall clearly knew more than a thing or two about small-bore Foxes, and this one turned out to be as splendid a piece of bird-grassing machinery as he had no doubt envisioned. On a good day when concentration does not wane, the tongue is held just so, and a couple of mental fingers remain crossed, the gun is truly a magic wand. With, as chum Charlie assured me, plenty of seriously tall reach.

A couple or so fall and winter seasons ago, a classy English girl caught my eye and managed to steal away a part of my heart. From one of London's best families, her original fluid steel tubes, outside hammers, and straight-hand stock were— simply put and with no defense implied—beyond resisting.

However, what was really never more than a mere dalliance has now run its course. The realization occurred to

---

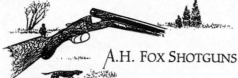

J.T. CALLAHAN
ARMS HISTORIAN

53 Old Quarry Road

Westfield, MA 01085

A.H. FOX SHOTGUNS

SAVAGE
STEVENS
A.H. FOX

Classic Sporting Images
Attn. William Headrick

May 7, 2003

Dear Mr. Headrick,

Thank you for writing concerning another interesting A.H. Fox double barrel shotgun.

This past week, I had the opportunity to search the factory serial records and locate the original record card for this shotgun bearing S/N 200644. The record card tells us that it was originally made as follows:

Grade- AE Grade
Gauge- 20 Gauge
Barrels- 30", choked Full and Full
Stock- Walnut(likely European), 14-1/4 length of pull, 1-7/8 drop at comb, 3" drop at heel, half pistol grip
Weight- 6 lb, 8 oz (specified) finished at 6 lb., 10 oz.
Notes- RUSH, No safety, No engraving on action or barrels, Select nice stock, must be exactly as ordered.

This double was completed at the A.H. Fox, Philadelphia plant and shipped on July 7, 1914. The original consignee is recorded as either "A" or "R" MacDougall. No address or location is provided on the card.

The "A" grade was first in a line of graded shotguns offered by the A.H. Fox Gun Co. I have stumbled on other odd Fox shotguns in the records that have been entered as "A" Grade guns for what I believe to be accounting or cost purposes. This shotgun is truly a special and is described and speculated about in McIntosh's book "A.H. Fox , The Finest Gun In The World". From what information you have given, this shotgun was built expressly for durability, function and hard use. It is evident that the original owner's concern was not for embellishment but for practicality in the shooting discipline for which he had it built.

I trust that this information is useful and helpful to you.

Sincerely,

John T. Callahan

John T. Callahan

3694/jtc

Factory-type letter based on 200644's production record.

the very lad to run it by was already enroute with preparations for his favorite supper well in the works.

McIntosh still lived in Missouri back then, and could be on our doorstep at the drop of a hat. More often it took the promise of a morning's wingshoot, a few good meals, an evening of billiards, some fair to middling whiskey, a pair of puppy ears to

FOX GUN
"The Finest Gun in the World"

A FOX GETS THE GAME

Becoming difficult to find in any condition, this 1914 large-format "A Fox Gets The Game" catalogue almost went missing its tipped-on front cover illustration. Below: Color copy 200644's shop card.

me during 200644's here-seen photo shoot. Increasingly, over a period of days, I found myself smoothly sweeping her rapier tubes and narrow muzzles through the imagined flight line of various objects within the studio. As often as not, after following a hapless decoy's or shell box's or doorknob's long and dead-in-the-air descent to earth, a rich and well-known baritone, delivered with flawless timing and an impeccable Highland brogue, would come to me from somewhere seemingly nearby:

"Aarrgghh…bro, yer bonnie MacDougall reached a far piece indeed to fetch that wee laddie she did now. Aye she did. Aarrgghh…"

With the recent arrival of our dove opener invitations, there is no doubt about which gal will once again be on my arm. And rest assured that she will be the belle of the ball. Just ask anyone who knows her.

Acknowledgements: The foregoing was written, photographed, and is here dedicated to the memory of Mr. Charles Wroten—resource person extraordinaire and good friend, now long missed and never to be forgotten.

The following individuals provided assistance: Dick Bangert, John Callahan, Roe Clark, John Iacopi, Ken Levin, David Noreen, and Gerald Schrader.

Resources: Michael McIntosh, A.H. Fox: "The Finest Gun In The World" (Traverse City: Countrysport Press, 1992 and 1994); various Fox catalogues and other company-produced advertising appropriate to the period; and archival materials preserved and maintained by the Savage-Stevens-Fox Corporation.

PHOTOGRAPH BY WILLIAM HEADRICK

Announcing The Launch Of
Roosevelt AND Drake

I am proud to announce the launch of a new company, Roosevelt and Drake. Building on Lewis Drake's reputation as one of America's premier vintage sporting gun dealers and taking its inspiration from my great grandfather's tradition as an outdoorsman, a hunter, and a conservationist, this new business will supply the highest quality products, with the least negative effect upon the environment to ethical and responsible hunters and other lovers of the outdoors.

We intend to re-create products and services similar to those that were available in Theodore Roosevelt's time. For example, in the eighteenth and nineteenth centuries, the great British furniture companies such as Hepplewhite, Sheraton, and Chippendale redesigned some of their finest furniture and created "breakdown" or "campaign" versions for their military officers and colonists. This beautiful and useful outdoor furniture has largely been forgotten, but once again will be available through Roosevelt and Drake. The unique and timeless functionality of this extraordinary furniture is equally appropriate for the finest office settings, the most rugged outdoor hunting camp, or your favorite rooms at home.

We will also offer a line of leather goods and shooting sports accessories of a variety and quality not available elsewhere. These include leather hunting bags, gun cases, hand-forged Damascus steel knives, a wide assortment of other useful and lovely outdoor acccessories, as well as period and contemporary clothing, all designed to the exacting standards of eighteenth century British sportsmen.

In order to guarantee quality equal to these standards, we manufacture virtually all of our products in our own shops. This attention to detail and quality has earned Roosevelt and Drake a reputation as one of the world's leading suppliers to the most sophisticated and discerning outdoors aficionado.

In addition to our unique selection of vintage firearms we will, from time to time, be introducing limited production shotguns and rifles of our own. Our first offering, to be unveiled at the Vintage Cup Shoot this fall in New York, will be the Roosevelt and Drake Round Action shotgun, a true trigger-plate action side by side with all the inherent advantages of that design including lightweight, superior strength, and sleek lines, and will have the added feature of a hand-detachable lock and trigger mechanism. These magnificent shotguns will be manufactured exclusively for Roosevelt and Drake by the highly respected firm of Famars di Abbiatico and Salvinelli and will be available on special order to our customers' exacting specifications.

Roosevelt and Drake will also make available the services of personally vetted superior outfitters from around the world so our clients may enjoy the very best in a wide variety of unusual outdoors experiences.

Our primary goal is to provide only what would have satisified Theodore Roosevelt's very high standards. All our products and services will be backed with a 100 percent satisfaction guarantee, and a no questions asked return policy.

TR once wrote, "I am not disposed to undervalue outdoor sports, or to fail to appreciate the advantage to a nation, as well as to an individual, of such pastimes." We intend to contribute to the continuation of this tradition. We are very much looking forward to a long and enjoyable relationship with the many people who love the outdoors as we do.

"...to provide only what would have satisfied Theodore Roosevelt's very high standards."

Tweed Roosevelt
www.rooseveltanddrake.com
270-753-7200

Book Review by Steve Bodio
The Paintings of Eldridge Hardie: Art of a Life in Sport

(Mechanicsburg , PA: Stackpole Books, 2002)

Eldridge Hardie is a fortunate man. He seems to have done everything there is to be done in the worlds of fly fishing and bird shooting, delighted in every moment, and returned to remind us how it is. If we are never as happy as we are in the field, recollecting our moments there in tranquility may be a close second. And Hardie stands tall among our contemporaries in his ability to capture these moments and moods.

This book is an elegant and comprehensive collection of Hardie and his human and canine protagonists doing what they love. You will see classic northern grouse hunting, the kind that still makes me nostalgic twenty-some years after it has been a regular part of my life; dove shooting, geese and ducks dropping into winter fields and ponds; classic two-mule quail wagons on a bobwhite plantation in Georgia; famous salmon rivers and bonefish flats; leaping tarpon, driven grouse in Scotland; a frozen pointer as hard-edged as a bronze sculpture. You will also see less common subjects, ones I have rarely seen in "sporting" paintings: Kansas prairies at dusk, quail in southern Arizona, chukar flushing over the depths of a canyon in western Colorado's rimrock country.

But that's just subject—necessary, but not sufficient to evoke the emotions that Hardie's paintings do. Hardie has studied the masters, mastered his sports, and used his eyes and hands until he has mastered his craft. Then and only then comes art, which is why it is all too seldom achieved. In Hardie's best paintings you look on the familiar with wonder, seeing it as something new.

In his introduction, George Reiger objects, mildly , to comparing Hardie to Ogden Pleissner. I see no problem. In subject you can compare him to Pleissner or Reneson, in his mastery of still water or leaping fish to old masters like Homer or Eakins. But he has taken in all the influences and come up with visions of his own.

I think he shines brightest at his most impressionistic. Consider *Two in the Hand*, a little (seven by ten inch, reproduced "life-sized") oil of a hunter, homeward bound on a curved road of mud and snow with pheasants in hand and a Lab by his side. It is simple, with bold brush strokes, a plain palette, and no calendar-like "detail." It is also, as the always perceptive painter Tom Daly says of another simple composition, "spare, clean… poignant, and memorable," as the end of a day afield should seem.

Look also at the painting Daly likes, *A Pheasant in a Plum Thicket;* at *Miramichi Fishing Canoe* (another tiny oil); at the arrow of a trout cutting the current in *Rising Brown Trout*. All these show what a master can do to suggest stillness or sudden motion by using paint to suggest light. They are the essence of impressionism.

Or if you like landscapes, look at his stark evocations of Kansas farm country, like *Franktown Barns* (a ranch hand told him "we were getting ready to tear that old barn down. I guess I never looked at it that way.") Or, another personal favorite, *Sundown Doves*, flighting in at the windmill at last light. Or *Early Risers*, a dawn study of a fisherman at a prairie pond in Colorado, with an orange sun burning through the mist and a heron gliding by. All these are watercolors—perhaps the medium best suited to subtle skies, to dusk and dawn.

Action? How about *Water Walker—Tarpon*, an explosion worth of, but very different from, Winslow Homer's leaping fish? Or the *On Scenic Mesa* painting of Colorado chukar and dogs I mentioned before, where the chasm suggested to the right combines with the springer leaping towards it to create apprehension as well as anticipation.

Portraits? My favorite is a soft watercolor of a cock Gambel's quail. Was he really only sixteen when he painted it?

A bonus*, unusual in painting books, is a rear section called "The Act" in which Hardie shows, with extracts from his field books, how much thought goes into a painting to make it seem so natural. He shows pencil sketches blocking out planes, watercolor sketches showing balance and shape, and notes to himself: "accents—2 white dogs—lt. On tree trunks—patch of water." To a non-artist, it is a reminder of how much work goes into looking effortless. Any fan of hunting dogs, game birds, double guns, fighting fish, water, dawn, sunset, and the sporting tradition will enjoy this book. Artists will find it both inspirational and, perhaps, instructional as well.

*Editor's note: Also See "A Sporting Artist's Thoughts On Making Pictures," DGJ, Autumn 1999, page 89.

Nicaragua
The Newest Wingshooting Frontier

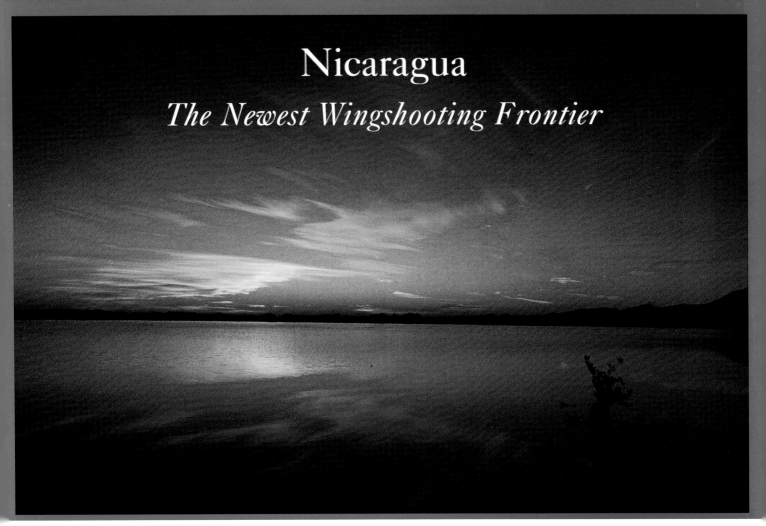

*Written and Photographed
by Stuart M. Williams*

I confessed to my friend Alfredo Pellas that I had never been to Nicaragua and knew virtually nothing about the country. On hearing that confession he immediately invited me to come to Nicaragua as his guest—in fact he insisted on it. To sweeten the invitation he told me all about the excellent bird shooting that was available there. He explained that during the winter months vast lagoons and swamps swarm with great flocks of blue-winged teal and with lesser numbers of shovellers and fulvous tree ducks. He went on to say that there are large numbers of white-winged doves in the corn and sorghum fields. He didn't have to twist my arm to get me to accept his invitation.

The date for our trip was set for early February 2001. A quick check of the lunar calendar revealed that the period fell squarely during the full moon—the worst possible time for a duck hunt. I pointed that out to Alfredo, who dis-missed my concern with the statement: "I have *always* had good duck hunting in Nicaragua—regardless of the timing—and besides I made plans for that time long ago and can't change them now." So I went ahead, against my better judgement.

I flew down from Miami to Managua with Alfredo Pellas and a business associate of his, Rafael Sanchez, another expatriate Nicaraguan hunter. Upon arrival we were greeted by still another expatriate—this one an American living in Nicaragua —Marvin Townsend, who is the only outfitter in Nicaragua. Marvin quickly took charge of our guns upon arrival and whisked them and our other luggage through customs in minutes and we were underway to the sumptuous Camino Real Hotel.

Marvin quickly took charge of our guns and whisked them and our other luggage through customs in minutes, and we were underway to the sumptuous Camino Real Hotel.

Unfortunately, due to the full moon, the teal shooting was

*A magical sunrise on the Nicaraguan marsh.
Inset: The pool house at the very elegant and comfortable Hotel Colonial in Grenada, where we stayed several days.*

Alfredo Pellas in a state of dove shooting bliss.
Below: When not shooting, we enjoyed the Nicaraguan markets—a feast for both eyes and palate.

not up to par, but in spite of that the experience was delightful. I shot in an idyllic situation, namely, a vast shallow lagoon densely overgrown with brilliant pink hyacinths from shore to shore and surrounded by steep, rough hills armored with high thorn trees, all under a cerulean sky filled with big marshmallow clouds. In the distance stood two gaunt volcanoes.

After the shoot we drove about an hour through a fertile valley to a town called Chinandega, where we would make our headquarters. Along the way we saw vast plantations of bananas and coffee bushes and large herds of cattle. We checked in at Hotel Los Volcanes, a pleasant tropical resort.

After lunch and a much-needed siesta we drove to a spot directly between the two volcanoes mentioned earlier and took up stands under big thorn trees amidst dense thorn brush and waited for white-

winged doves. The action was slow to start, but when it finally arrived it was so frenetic that I simply couldn't load and fire fast enough to keep up with the birds. To complicate matters, a side wind was gusting up to 25 mph and the birds were swerving in and out and around the trees, presenting difficult targets. I have always said that windblown doves are the most difficult targets and here was ample proof. I got 60 birds with seven boxes of shells, which I considered to be quite respectable.

The next morning we shot doves in rolling brown fields bordered by stands of high tropical hardwood trees. It was a beautiful setting—gentle breezes, brilliant sunshine, cool temperatures, and the fragrance of wildflowers wafting around us.

Next we enjoyed one of the high points of the trip, a visit to Alfredo Pellas' sugar mill. It processes

My brother Tom boards the boat for a trip to the duck-shooting platform.

sugarcane from a plantation of about 35,000 acres.

Afterwards Marvin put on a very exciting dove shoot. He placed us in the shade of a dense row of tall eucalyptus with our backs to the trees. I was situated between Dr. Rodney Baine, a surgeon from Mississippi, and Oscar Zaladana, a very successful entrepreneur from El Salvador. A 20–25 mph wind blew at our backs. On our left—to the west—loomed the gaunt silhouettes of the ever-present volcanoes. In front of us lay a field of harvested sorghum. The birds flew across that field and over the eucalyptus trees, flying to their roosts in the rough brushy hills behind us. They were the very soul of evasiveness. They performed every aerobatic maneuver imaginable and were certainly some of the most difficult birds I had ever shot. I had only 35 birds picked up, but under the circumstances

that number was extremely satisfying. That was the way I would have wanted to end up the shooting portion of the trip, and that is the way I did end it.

It was over all too soon, so when Alfredo Pellas insisted that we come again, we readily accepted.

I went back in January 2003, precisely during the dark of the moon. I wasn't taking any chances this time. Accompanying me were some of my old worldwide wingshooting buddies—Dr. E.P. Couch; and attorney Greg Nellis of Tulsa, Oklahoma; Bob Griffiths, a construction magnate from San Francisco; and my brother T.C. Williams, a Wall Street investment banker. We were joined by Paolo Coen, a prominent businessman with interests throughout Central America, with whom I had shot driven pheasants in Hungary.

After two days in Managua we drove north to Chinandega. We passed long vistas of palm and acacia trees and fencerows flaming with orange and red bougainvillea and dormant volcanoes framing Lake Managua in the distance. At last we arrived at Hotel Las Mananitas, which would be our headquarters for the next three days. It was a charming, simple place, surrounded by palm trees and bougainvillea, with an al fresco bar area and an elegant dining room.

The following morning, however, was the morning we had been waiting for. The airboat transported us to our blinds, threading its way through a labyrinth of channels cut through ten-foot-tall tules. I bagged twenty-six ducks—five blue-winged teal and twenty-one fulvous tree ducks.

I shot red hot that morning. Hundreds and hundreds of tree ducks milled about aimlessly high overhead, but periodically a big group would fly just within gunning range. Almost all the shots were straight overhead against a deep turquoise sky—my favorite shot. It was a bluebird day, without a breath of breeze or a cloud in the sky, the kind of day when ducks just don't fly without some encouragement. The airboats provided precisely that encouragement.

Afterwards we roared around through the channels of the marsh until we had collected every duck, then went back to the boat landing and swapped lies about our great shooting. That was a big part of the pleasure. Bob Griffiths was high gun for the morning with thirty ducks recovered.

Then we moved a short distance away to a temporary encampment, where Marvin's boys had set up a folding table and chairs under a huge shade tree. Two cooks were grilling thick steaks and dove and duck breasts and big sausages over an open fire, and the air was full of irresistible aromas. Soon the cooks were ladling out big portions of rice and beans and serving huge slabs of steaks and the grilled birds and sausages. They prepared far more than we could eat.

Afterwards we moved father back into the shade where hammocks had been hung among the trees. There we took a profound siesta among the most wonderful breezes!

That afternoon we enjoyed one of the unique pleasures of Nicaragua, a visit to a cigar factory. The factory we visited was called Tobaccos Plasencia in Esteli. From the moment we entered the door we were exhilarated by the heady fragrance of fine cigars. We saw the whole works: drying and deep-freezing of leaves, fermentation and

Once shooters are in position, the boats move through brilliant water hyacinths to flush the ducks.

aging, rolling, wrapping, trimming, gauging, sorting by color, wrapping in cellophane, and packaging. In the antiseptic workrooms an atmosphere of total concentration prevailed. Hardly a word was spoken.

The next day was the last duck hunt and the last hurrah. My

A view of Hotel Las Mananitas,
our headquarters while in Chinandega.

shooting platform was situated along a channel about sixty yards wide. On either side of the channel reeds formed a solid green wall ten feet high. Huge trees leaned far out over the water on which floated great lily pads with pink and white flowers.

Volleys of teal traded back and forth along this channel, some low,

Oscar Zaldana safely boards the boat
after a wonderful morning duck shoot.

Admiral's Lodge on Ometepe Island; one of the most paradisical places I have ever visited.
Below: The "Admiral," Pedro Chamorro with a couple of nice guapote we caught.

some quite high. I saw thousands in the course of the shoot. The shots presented were all difficult, either because the ducks were far out or high up. I fired my entire allotment of four boxes of shells and killed about sixty ducks.

One of the unusual things about this shoot was that about half the ducks I shot were shovellers. Never let anyone scorn the sporting qualities of the much-maligned shoveller. It is as fast and evasive as any mallard.

We enjoyed a superb lunch at Paolo Coen's lavish ranch nearby. In the shade of an elegant luncheon pavilion, laved by delicious breezes, we feasted on grilled pork steak, chicken, and beef, purple cabbage salad, and more refried beans.

That evening Paolo arranged a horse show, which was a wonderful way to end the trip. We watched from inside a beautiful enclosed grandstand and saw horsemanship that would rival anything you might see at the Spanish Riding School in Vienna.

And so the shooting trip came to an end.

Afterwards, I headed out on a fishing excursion to Admiral's Lodge on Ometepe Island in Lake Nicaragua, a spot Mark Twain visited as a young man and later wrote about. We fished for guapote which are caught by trolling with deep-running lures and which are known for their tableworthiness. Ometepe Island is the largest lake island in the world and truly a place of unearthly beauty…a paradise indeed and to go there was a fitting end to a wonderful trip and my adventures in Nicaragua—the new frontier.

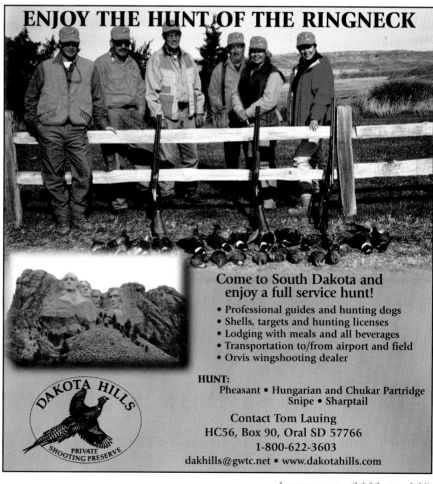

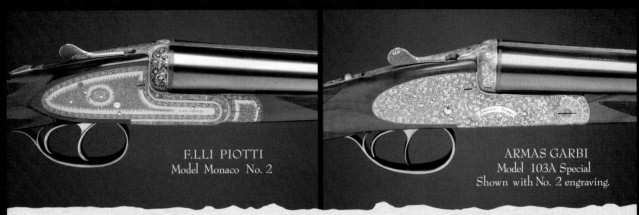

Horsley No. 2196
Something Old, Something New

Written and Photographed
by David J. Baker

You know how it is, the gun just winked at me! Why this one out of all the other Horsleys? Well, the fact that it's a 16 bore makes it just a touch neater and somehow prettier than the usual 12 and, in large measure, the honest, used condition it was in appealed to me. If we are realistic, the chance of finding a truly mint shotgun over 100 years old is about on a par with winning a major lottery prize. You are much more likely to see a resuscitated specimen which, alas, so often means it has been on the receiving end of the handiwork of a "garage gunsmith" who thinks he can checker and who has a big wire brush on his electric drill.

So the combination of crisp, undamaged metalwork, with the honest dirt of lots of use, and woodwork with the patina that comes also

Hon. John Charles Dundas, Jr.
(1845–1892)

with use was simply great. We all have our own ideas on what is acceptable in terms of restoration; mine can be summed up as a gentle, but thorough clean and little more. That said, 2196 presents a rather different problem. I am certain that, sometime in the fairly distant past, it has been refurbished, probably by Smith's of Retford, whose oval stamp can just be deciphered on the left-hand side of the stock. The most obvious sign of this refurbishment is a new hinge pin which, of course, explains why this 129-year-old gun is so tight. The greater problem derives from this revamping in that the metalwork was almost certainly given a lick of quick blue. Just how much of a quick touch-up is betrayed by the presence of a disc of bright metal under the head of the screws holding

*Stamp of "West of Retford" at left side of stock.
At left: Proof Exemption Certificate
from Birmingham Proof House.*

Proof Exemption Certificate

issued by

The Birmingham Gun Barrel Proof House

Banbury Street, Birmingham B5 5RH

CAVENDO   *TUTUS*

I hereby certify that the gun, or other small arm, details of which are set out below, has been submitted to this Proof House today, but has not or cannot be proved because:-

The arm is an antique or collector's piece, which is not intended to be fired, is unlikely to withstand the proof test and might be severely damaged if subjected to proof.

Type and Make: **Double Barrel Shotgun - T.Horsley**

Gauge, Chamber Length or Calibre: **16 Bore x 65mm**

Number: **2196**   Barrel Length: **29.5"**

Other Identifying Features, Invalid Proof Marks etc.

Submitted by: **John Dillon (Gun Repairs)**

CGPE No. **673**

Private view mark impressed   Date: **19/12/02**

PROOF MASTER
for the Guardians of the Birmingham Proof House

WARNING:- The arm, to which this certificate should be attached, must not be offered for sale as serviceable. It has not been proved and should not be fired.

the hammers. What to do with this finish was a problem. In so far as it was applied during the working life of the gun, it has some legitimacy, but again it is not the right sort of finish. After some deliberation, I realized I could rub off the quick blue, matching the exposed metalwork to the finish surviving on the untreated parts. It is, of course, a matter of opinion, but I feel I have achieved an appearance which is very close to how the gun would have looked had it never been quick blued.

One area where the re-blue is no real problem is the barrels, because they are steel. This is not the earliest pair of Horsley steel barrels I have encountered, those were sold in 1868. Unfortunately, there is no indication on either pair of barrels as to what sort of steel they were made of. Oddly, in both cases, the word "steel" is stamped on the bottom rib. This is a shame, because a greater description might have helped to explain the next oddity on this gun. As it stands now, it is way out of proof. The bores measure .685 and .684, which means that they have lost approximately two thousandths of an inch in their wall thickness. I suspect this was done when 2196 was refurbished. Then folks did not bother about such technicalities as proof laws! What is much more remarkable is that 9 inches from the breech face the barrel walls are still some 28–30 thousandths of an inch thick. So, when new, there must have been massive wall thickness. I wonder if someone did not trust steel! Another facet to this part of the story is that now the wall thickness drops to 19 and to 17 thousandths of an inch out at 6 inches from the muzzle. I wonder if this was done to enhance the balance of the gun. Just think what it would have been like if it had been manufactured with huge barrel-wall thickness out to the muzzles.

The barrels present another problem because, on paper at least, it looks as if they would stand re-proof. Tempting of course, especially as the bores are almost perfect inside. The snag is that thin muzzle portion which, while probably safe, would be vulnerable to dents. Then there is the fact that the bar-in-wood Horsley action

Underside of 2196 showing grip safe lever.

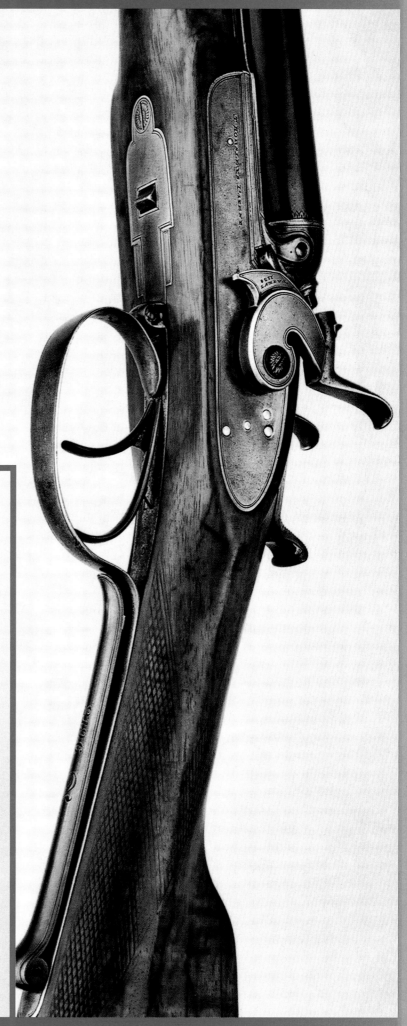

doesn't have a lot of "meat" in it. I know others of this ilk have stood Nitro proof. The question really came down to did I need another 16 bore to shoot or did I want to be certain of keeping this Horsley intact?

Since I have just had a sweet little 16-bore Dickson go through Nitro, I could not claim to need another 16. So, I have gone the "proof exemption certificate" route. That makes 2196 legal to sell in Great Britain. I think that this is the right

tion, which has obviously functioned flawlessly throughout the gun's long life. Now I know of several Horsleys that were made with grip safeties, but the great majority do not have these devices now. I am certain that they get removed because, on some examples, it is possible to grip the gun in such a way that the safety stays on when the shot is attempted. I am sure that 2196 is still as it was made, because it has the broad, long lever under the hand of the stock. This was

"Steel" is stamped on the bottom rib of Horsley No. 2196.

way to go, because I believe this 16-bore Horsley is well worthy of preservation. Not just because it is a 16 and they are unusual, but because of its mechanical features, which make it possible to get a proof exemption certificate on this gun. The proof authorities will only grant a certificate on what they term "a collector's item," which, for them, means a gun that is mechanically unusual. They do not, yet at least, accept that a gun can be collectable by reason of its provenance. It seems that each candidate is judged on its merits, since there is neither protocol nor published guidance leaflet. Although the Birmingham Proof House tells me that they do keep a record of the gun to which exemption has been granted.

In some respects, the proof exemption scheme could be regarded as unsatisfactory but, in practice, it has been a huge boon to the collecting fraternity of Great Britain. Prior to its inception, in the "real world," out of proof but interesting guns were traded on a "nod and wink" basis, with both parties aware that, technically, they were breaking the law. Now, with a proof exemption certificate, such guns can be sold legally at auction or openly offered for sale in a shop, which is, of course, better for all concerned.

Perhaps the most obvious feature qualifying this Horsley for its certificate is a grip safety in perfect working condi-

the original form as described in Matthew Watt's patent of 1818. With a lever of this shape, it is practically impossible to grip the gun in such a way that you could control the recoil and not avoid pulling the trigger.

How these safeties work is very simple. On the inside of the trigger plate there is a spring-loaded, rocking lever, set up so that the front end of the lever butts against the rear of the trigger blades and prevents the triggers from swinging on their pivots. All that the upward projection from the external safety lever has to do is lift the rear of the internal lever so that the front portion no longer bears on the trigger blades. Beautifully simple and, as this specimen demonstrates, a device that will work faultlessly for a century or more.

Problems with this system occur when, in the interests of neatness, the large external lever is replaced by a short, narrow blade that does not project far from the tang of the trigger guard. In this manifestation, it is possible for the blade to get lost in the hand, so it is not squeezed enough.

A feature of 2196 is the design of the locks, perhaps less immediately obvious than the grip safety, but of even more significance in the overall story of the Horsley gun. From the records we know that this gun was sold new in 1874, well within the period of the rebound lock. Yet the gun is

Wingshooting Adventures
with
Jack J. Jansma & Son
O-1845 West Leonard
Grand Rapids, Michigan 49544-9510 U.S.A.

NEW ARRIETA SIDELOCKS IN STOCK
We have over 40 Arrietas in stock ready for delivery, every gauge available, pairs in 12 and singles.

MODEL 557 2" 12 ga. 27" barrels choked Skt1/IC. 14-3/4" LOP. Nice wood. 5 lbs. 14 ozs.................**$4,050**
MODEL 570 2" 12 ga. 27" barrels choked Skt1/IC. 14-3/4" LOP. Well figured wood............................**$4,650**
MODEL 570 16 ga. 28" barrels choked Skt1/IC. 14-3/4" LOP. Well figured wood..............................**$4,650**
MODEL 578 20 ga. 28" barrels choked IC/M. Rounded action..**$5,200**
MODEL 557 20 ga. 28" barrels choked IC/M **$4,200**
MODEL 570 .410 ga. 29" barrels,rounded action, SC 14-3/4" LOP. Well figured wood.......................**$5,050**
MODEL 578 16 ga. 28" barrels choked IC/M, 14-3/4" LOP. Well figured wood...............................**$5,050**
MODEL 557 12 ga. 29" barrels choked IC/M. 14-3/4" LOP. Very well figured stock **$3,950**
MODEL 578 28 ga. 29" barrels choked IC/M. Upgraded wingshooter wood **$5,050**
MODEL 578 12 ga. 29" barrels choked Skt.2/IM 6 lbs. 12 ozs. Nice wood **$4,650**
MODEL 803 20 ga. 28" barrels choked M/F..**$7,000**
MODEL 871 2" 12 ga. 29" barrels choked Skt1/Skt2. Awesome wood! **$5,000**
MODEL 801 20 ga. 28" barrels choked IC/M, ST **$9,050**
MODEL 872 12 ga. *USED.* 30" barrels choked IC/M 15-1/4" LOP to leather pad, 99%. New cost is over $13,700!! **$7,950**

MATCHED PAIRS

ARRIETA 802 (Pre-owned) 12 ga., 27" barrels, DT SGS. Very nice wood, cased **$9,500**
ARRIETA 803 20 ga. 28" barrels choked Skt2/F. AAA fancy wood **$15,000**
ARRIETA 578 12 ga., 29" barrels choked IC/M. Great wood. (2 pairs in stock new).........................**$11,000**
HELLIS BLE 28" barrels choked IC/F. The wood on this pair is outstanding, in a newer case with proper label .**$10,000**
BEESLEY SLE 12 ga. 30" barrels, ST choked F/IC. Oak and leather case, outstanding wood.
Some case color remaining...**$25,000**
PURDEY 2" 12 ga. 28" barrels, **Lightweights.** Very rare pair! Call us for details **$70,000**
Purdey has assured us that less than 20 pairs of 2" 12 gauge were ever produced, the last pair of 2" 12 Purdeys sold at auction for more than $65,000 (2000). The wood on our pair is simply outstanding. These shotguns were made for Lord Marshall in 1934. The chokes are original to factory, as is the barrel wall thickness. Original case. 90% case coloring. King Ranch shotguns.

ENGLISH OFFERINGS

PURDEY 12 ga. 30" and 27" barrels, rounded action, cased, AAA wood, 75% case color. c. 1954 ....**$35,000**
MACNAUGHTON 20 ga. 2-1/2" 28" barrels (NPD) bar in wood non-ejector. Original condition. Cased .....**SOLD!**
GRANT 12 ga. 2-1/2" 30" barrels. Very nice piece of wood. Top lever. Some case coloring **$10,000**
ALEXANDER HENRY 12 ga. 28" barrels. Game scene. Awesome wood, cased.................................**$6,950**
BOSS 20 ga. O/U 26" barrels IC/M, DT, 95% original case coloring. Case with all the goodies. Fabulous!..**$70,000**
BOSS 20 ga. SxS 25" barrels ST 100% original case colors. Original untouched Boss 20. With paperwork .**SOLD!**

OTHER FINE SHOTGUNS

ITHACA Classic Double 28 ga. 30" and 28" barrels Custom Exhibition Grade, made in 2000. Cased **$15,000**
WINCHESTER 21 20 gauge 28" barrels, M/F ST, beavertail, PGS 100% condition **$6,000**
BROWNING M1 20 gauge 28" barrels three piece forend. Very highly figured straight stock **$18,500**
BROWNING M2 20 gauge 26" barrels three piece forend. Very highly figured straight stock **$15,500**
PERAZZI MX28 28" barrels with multi-chokes SCO wood. Cased **$6,000**

Our hours of operation are 9 a.m.–5 p.m. Eastern. We are available by appointment only. Please feel free to call!
We do take appointments on Saturday and Sunday.
2003 shoots are filling up fast! We are now offering a Spring "Gran Chaco Pigeon" shoot in Paraguay
beginning in 2003. This shoot has been one of our favorites. It is pigeon shooting at its very finest.
We have brochures and videos available for our Hungarian, Scottish, and Spanish driven bird shoots. We have been
doing these for a number of years and have broken some price barriers that will interest you. If you have ever had
the desire to participate in this "sport of kings," PLEASE CALL FOR DETAILS!
For the most up-to-date gun list, please visit our Web-site: www.wingshootingadv.com

Phone (616) 677-1980   "Importer of Arrieta Sidelock Double Shotguns"   Fax (616) 677-1986

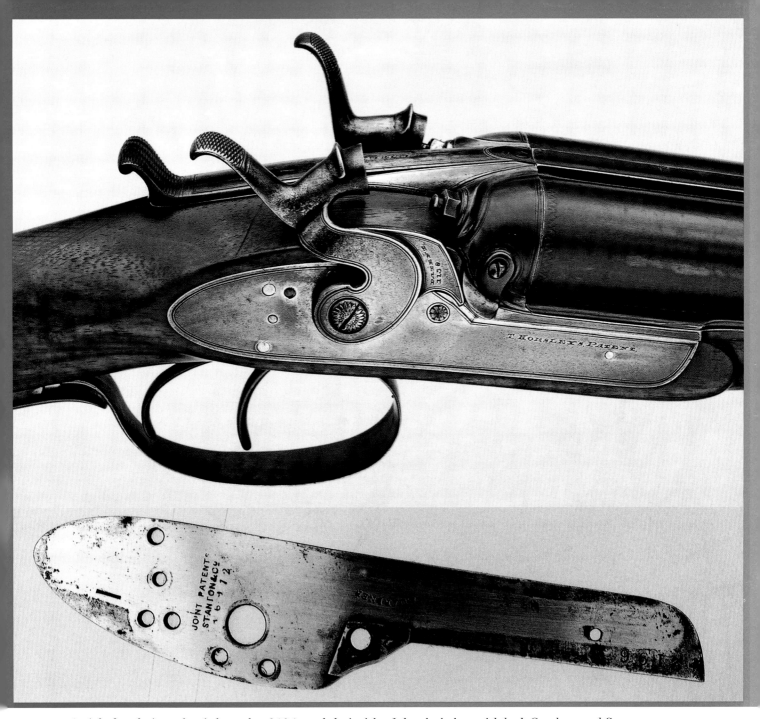

A right-hand view of serial number 2196, and the inside of that lockplate with both Gardner and Stanton stamps.

fitted with mechanically retracting firing pins as well as rebound locks. Now the conventional view is that the rebound lock, which caused the hammer to come to rest off the firing pin, did away with the need to retract pins mechanically. There are other Horsleys known that have rebound locks and retracting firing pins, but the question has always been, were the locks made like this or were they converted? This is a valid question, since locks were converted wholesale to the new system and, if the work was done to the standard of the original, for practical purposes it is impossible to detect.

Things are different on 2196. When the locks are removed, you see the maker's name, "A. Gardner," in the characteristic curved stamp. I am almost certain that Albert Gardner was Horsley's in-house lockmaker, because I have seen and handled the punch that made that mark and was told, on the best authority, that it was found in the "junk"

when Horsley's shop was cleared. Moreover, Albert is listed in the 1881 census living at 7 Clarence Street, in the parish of St. Giles, while the dates and places of the births of his children suggest that he moved to York after 1873.

When I stripped the locks to clean them, I made another discovery. Under the tumbler, invisible when the lock is assembled, is another stamp, this time "Joint Patent John Stanton & Co." This must mean that these locks were made within the span of the 1867 patent and that Horsley or Gardner paid a royalty to use this system. What exactly the A6-72 means is a matter for speculation. Perhaps this was how this payment was arranged, or indeed monitored. It is possible that this is some evidence of the links Gardner must have maintained with the gun-lock centre in "The Black Country," because it is almost certain that he would have bought parts for his locks as rough forgings and stampings, which were then filed and polished to become the jewels that lurk inside the lockplates.

So, there is little doubt that the locks were originally made as we now see them. A careful look at the cams on the breasts of the hammers reveals that the camming surface is not a smooth curve as on earlier locks. Here there are two arcs which join roughly in the middle. Taking the lock through the firing sequence in slow motion reveals that, as the hammer rebounds, the top portion of the cam acts on the firing pin lever and so, in effect, the lock mainspring both half-cocks the lock and retracts the firing pin. This is a very neat, "belt and braces" approach to the question of safety, but one which was only used for a fairly short period—yet another twist to the Horsley story.

As always, part of the fun of finding a "new" Horsley is what I call the "head hunt," the search to find something about the original owner, with the ultimate hope of finding a portrait. At first glance, 2196 looked as if my quest should have been simple as it and 2195 had been sold to "Hon. J.C. Dundas." As in the way of such things, in reality the facts were more difficult. In short, he was the younger son of a youngest son, who was given the same Christian names as his father, none of which helps research. Luckily, things got better. His uncle died without an heir, so J.C.'s elder brother inherited, becoming the third Earl of Zetland. Better still, J.C. Dundas, Junior, became a Member of Parliament in 1873, sitting for Richmond, the seat having been vacated by his elder brother when he inherited the title.

I always nurture the hope that my original owners will be interesting "characters." What I have found so far paints John Charles as a pillar of society; he treated all his fellow men with respect and devoted himself to public service. On the event of his sudden death, there were the usual expressions of condolence. Now obituaries should always be approached with caution as they tend to stress the positive. In this instance, however, the long list of tributes from fellow magistrates published in the local paper have such a constant theme that more credence can be given to them. Typical of the accolades is this from a one-time political opponent: "His conduct was always that of an honorable, upright and conscientious man." Such men make a civilized society work. As a direct result of his civic work, I was able to obtain easily a splendid portrait and so add the finishing touch to my quest to put the gun into its historical context.

Finally, there is one more facet to the story of 2196. Soon after I had first seen it, I was talking to Peter Nelson about it and he reminded me of the gunmaker's motto "engraving hides the gunsmithing." On my long drive back to Wales, I mulled over this remark in the Horsley context. I just wonder if this might be the clue to the fact that there are many plain Horsley guns. Such guns are not unknown by other makers, but I am convinced that a greater proportion of Horsleys are border engraved. If Thomas Horsley thought along these lines, did he convey his thoughts to his customers? Did he plant the idea that a plain gun was right for a plain-speaking Yorkshire shooting man? The ideal was to create a fine gun with fine lines, devoid of frippery, following Beau Brummell's concept. I shall never know, of course, but the facts seem to fit the theory, which I will inevitably hereafter link to Peter Nelson and this particularly elegant product of the Coney Street workshop.

Note: For those who would like to know more about the family of the Honorable J.C. Dundas, go to "Zetland" on your internet search engine and click on "The Zetland Dundas."

FOWL WEATHER FRIEND
THE RUGER ALL-WEATHER® RED LABEL

NEW!
RUGER
12 GAUGE
TARGET GREY® ALL-WEATHER
RED LABEL SHOTGUN

KRLP-1227-TG

Suggested retail price of $1489.00

Nice weather for ducks all too often means wretched weather for duck hunters. Ruger now offers over-and-under shotguns that stand up to the worst that Mother Nature can hand out. Our new All-Weather Red Label shotguns feature stainless steel barrels and receivers, in your choice of brushed stainless or low-glare stainless Target Grey® models. Black synthetic stocks are strong, unobtrusive and absolutely weather-proof. The sleek, compact Ruger locking system is considered one of the strongest ever built for over-and-under shotguns. Back-boring reduces the felt recoil of heavy game loads and enhances pattern uniformity. It's the gun you'll want by your side especially when the weather isn't on your side.

STURM, RUGER & CO., INC.
Southport, CT 06890, U.S.A. • www.ruger.com
All Ruger firearms are designed and manufactured in our own factories in the United States of America.
FREE Instruction Manuals are now available online at www.ruger.com

RUGER®
ARMS MAKERS FOR RESPONSIBLE CITIZENS®

Robin Hollow Outfitters

*Dealers of
Fine Guns &
Sporting Accessories*

*See us for all of your needs,
including shooting attire,
accessories, gun fitting
and instruction.*

William Hadfield
President

www.robinhollow.com

Addieville East Farm
200B Pheasant Drive
Mapleville, RI 02839
Ph. 401-568-0331
Fax 401-568-0264

AMERICAN

Parker VHE 20 bore, 27-1/2" M/F shortened just a bit but a classic American bird gun **$2950**
Browning Superposed, superlight 20 ga., mint original condition to hard butt **$3,500**
Browning Superposed Midas, Lightning 20 bore, 28" SK/IC. Absolutely gorgeous and mint condition **$10,500**
Winchester M21s We have several, including No. 6 with gold, 20 ga.; No. 6 with gold, .410 and No. 6, 16 ga. Others also in stock. ....**Call for details**
Parker Reproductions Large selection of rare guns, including A1 Specials and BHE. Also some DHE. All unfired, in cases. ....**Call for prices**
Ithaca Grade 2, 20 ga., all original, excellent condition, game scenes, 26", semi-pistol grip, hard butt, beautiful little bird gun. **$2,850**
Ithaca Classic Doubles Very rare Exhibition Special, 28 ga., 2 bbl. set, 30" IC/M, 28", SKT/IC. 15" LOP to checkered butt, 5 lbs. 8 ozs., cased. **$16,950**
Parker Bros VH 28 ga. (mfg. 1902). Very early gun. All original with 26" bbls., dog's head butt, with factory letter.................................... **$6,500**
A.H. Fox AE 20 ga., 28", late engraving (deep relief) with factory beavertail, very hard to find American classic **$4,500**
Ithaca 4E trap/skeet combo, 12 ga., 32" F&F, 26" SKT/SKT, restored to new, leather case **$6,500**
Browning Midas 4 ga. skeet set (12, 20, 28, .410), mint condition, maker's case **$12,900**
Browning Belgian custom 2 bbl. set, game scene with gold inlays, 12 bore, mfg. 1958, absolutely beautiful engraving by A. Griebel **$13,950**
Winchester M-21 Tournament Skeet, 20 ga., mfg. 1935, nice wood, checkered butt, 26" WS1/WS2 ....**$7,500**

BRITISH

MacNaughton 28 ga. Damascus bird gun. English to stock, 4-1/2 lbs. with original 24" bbls., a fine little gun **$9,500**
Westley Richards Snap action boxlock, 1930s mfg. with bottom inspection, floor plate, excellent...**$4,950**
Mortimer & Son Boxlock ejector, 12 bore, 28" lightweight game gun, very nice bird gun, excellent..**$2,950**
J. Braddell & Son (Castle Place, Belfast) 16 ga., ejector gun, 28" bls., beautiful, 14-1/4" to thick pad..**$2,750**
Purdeys Only three 20-bore guns remain from collection. Gorgeous little guns in excellent condition. ....**From $39,000**
Cogswell & Harrison 16 bore, game gun, 28", excellent condition, maker's leather case and accessories **$3,950**
Joseph Lang & Son 12 bore, 28", very nice original condition, cased. **$9,800**
Henry Atkin Best sidelock, 12 bore, English stock, double triggers, classic dimensions, gorgeous, cased.............................**From $13,500**
Thomas Turner 12 ga., lightweight walk-up gun, 6 lbs., straight grip, splinter forend, scalloped action, full coverage engraving, ejectors, great little gun..**$3,500**
Joseph Lang Best sidelock, 16 ga., 28", English stock, very nice little gun..**$12,900**

Charles Lancaster sidelock, 12 bore, 28", IC/M, straight grip, 14-7/8" LOP, 100% coverage, beautifully engraved **$11,900**
Thomas Wild pigeon gun, 12-bore sidelock, 30", M/F, very nice wood, pistol grip, excellent condition **$14,900**
W.W. Greener 12 bore, very light game gun, 6 lbs. 28", metal and mechanical excellent, wood refinished, English stock, very nice. **$2,495**
Joseph Lang & Son sidelock, 12 bore, 28", very nice original condition **$9,800**

BRITISH RIFLES

Double Rifles by Joseph Lang and Westley Richards. 465/500, 450/400, 3-1/4"...**Call For Details**

EUROPEAN

Franchi Imperial Grade, 12 ga. Best sidelock, lightweight bird gun, 25" bbls., choke .005/.011, excellent mechanically but has been hunted and has stock extension. To order new today is $50,000, but this one is. **$2,500**
A&S Famars Best sidelock, 28 ga., 28", 5-1/2 lbs., engraved bulino game scene by Pedersoli, cased. **$20,000**
Beretta 451 EELL 12 bore, 28" set up for pigeon for clays, deluxe engraving, mint condition **$13,900**
Arrieta 578 Matched pair, 12 bore, 28", English stocks, hand-detach-able locks...**$9,500**
F.illi Poli Ivory deluxe, 28 ga., 28" IC/M, English stock, oil finish, case colors, beautiful little gun...**$3,700**
Famars We are taking orders for bespoke guns, and have several guns coming into our showroom for immediate delivery. These are some of the finest smooth bores the world has to offer.. ....**Call For Availability**
Famars Sovereign Grade, 12 bore, 30", magnificent deluxe ornamental engraving, exhibition wood, pinless sidelock. A best gun, new, maker's case **$47,500**
B. Rizzini We have a nice selection of these fine O/U field and sporting guns in stock. Upgraded wood and custom dimensions available. ....**From $1,950 to $8,500**
Arrieta 2", 12 ga., limited mfg., 5 lbs. 15 ozs., English stock, beautiful maker's case **$4,500**
We also have several other Arrietas in stock, all gauges.. ....**Call For Details**
Beretta 687 EELL Extra, 28 ga./.410 combo, 2 bbl. set. New in case with Exhibition wood. 28" bbls., factory chokes **$7,500**
Perazzi SC-3 field guns and sporting, 28", 29", 30"bbls., gorgeous, several from which to choose ....**$8,900–$10,900**
Beretta SO-5 Sporting, 12 bore, early gun, fast handling, 30", special-order stock, Mobile chokes...**$11,500**
LeBeau-Courally Best sidelock, 12 bore, 29", IC/M, English stock, beautiful engraving **$12,500**
N. Guyot/Francotte 12 bore, sideplates, 28", IC/M, English stock sideplates, 28", IC/M, English stock, 6 lbs. 4 ozs., 14-1/2" LOP. Best engraving..**$10,900**

All guns shipped have a 3-day inspection period that begins upon arrival via UPS/FedEx at intended destination (FFL dealer).

BRILEY'S JUST AN OVERGROWN MACHINE SHOP.

YEAH. RIGHT.

- • CHOKES •
- • TUBE SETS •
- • ACCESSORIES •
- • CUSTOM RIFLES •
- • CUSTOM PISTOLS •
- • ENGLISH DOUBLES – VINTAGERS HQ •
- • RUDY PROJECT SHOOTING GLASSES •
- • BARONEROSSO SHOOTING WEAR •
- • MATTARELLI TRAPS •
- • SPORTING & 5-STAND RENTAL •
- • ASKARI OUTDOOR GEAR & LUGGAGE •
- • AND MORE •

Relax and enjoy the finer things in life.
When in Houston,
visit our new retail store and showroom.
Briley.
1230 Lumpkin
Houston, Texas 77043
800-331-5718
www.briley.com

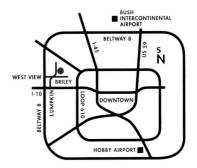

BRILEY
A Legacy of Shooting Innovation.

The Wilkes-Barre Gun Co.

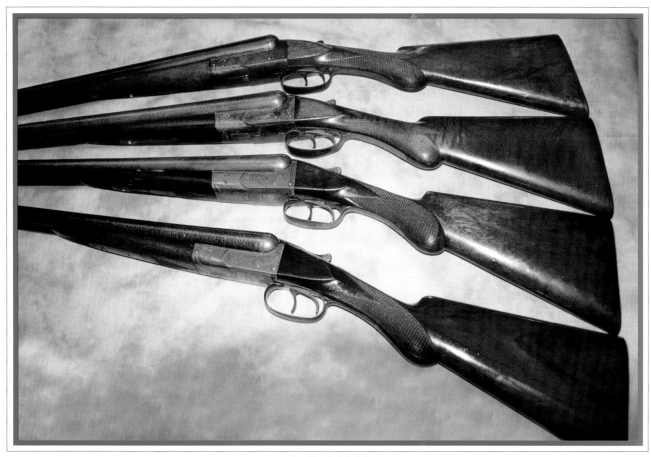

by Bob Noble
& William Achtermeier

Much has been written to fill in the mosaic that is the history of the American breech-loading double. Most collectors and arms students find easy identification with names such as Remington, Parker, Ithaca, Lefever, and Fox, but names such as A.J. Aubrey, Crescent, Iver Johnson, Meriden Fire Arms, Forehand and Wadsworth, Folsom, N.R. Davis, Clark and Sneider, and Kirkwood (to mention but a few) evoke little familiar response. Although spanning a tremendous gap in quality (and quantity), this latter grouping, nevertheless, represents an important part of that historical mosaic. Into this category can be placed the double guns produced by the short-lived Wilkes-Barre Gun Company, Wilkes-Barre, Pennsylvania.

Evolving out of the Parry Fire Arms Company of Ithaca, New York, the Wilkes-Barre Gun Company produced both hammer and hammerless doubles of varying grades. These double guns have often placed collectors in a quandary. Because of the lack of any factory records, estimates as to the number of doubles produced remain just that—estimates. The situation becomes even more opaque with the introduction of the question as to when Parry production ceased and Wilkes-Barre production began. The matter becomes further obscured by the possibility of what some collectors have long suspected—a double serial series.

The hint of an explanation is to be found in an article in the *Wilkes-Barre Record* for March 2, 1892:

> "Guns To Order
> Not cheap concerns, but guns equal
> to the highest price importations"

"'The man who doesn't know what he wants is the hardest sort of fellow to fit,' explained superintendent Collins of the South Wilkes-Barre Gun Works yesterday and he continued, 'the same rules apply to gun making as to all other mechanical productions. The user may think he knows how to shoot a gun, in fact he may think himself a good shot and yet not be aware of the fact that his misses arise from not knowing what his gun is capable of doing. A gun that is made to throw over 300 shot in a 24 inch target at 35 yards rise is a good enough weapon for a good shot, but many sportsmen think a gun should cover the whole visible horizon, then "what they hit is history but what they miss is mystery." Makers of good guns therefore test them, and if you care to go up I will show you how we give each purchaser of our gun its exact capacity,' and he at once led the way to the range which is in the loft

Pictured from top: The four grades of Wilkes-Barre hammerless shotguns, D, C, B, and A.

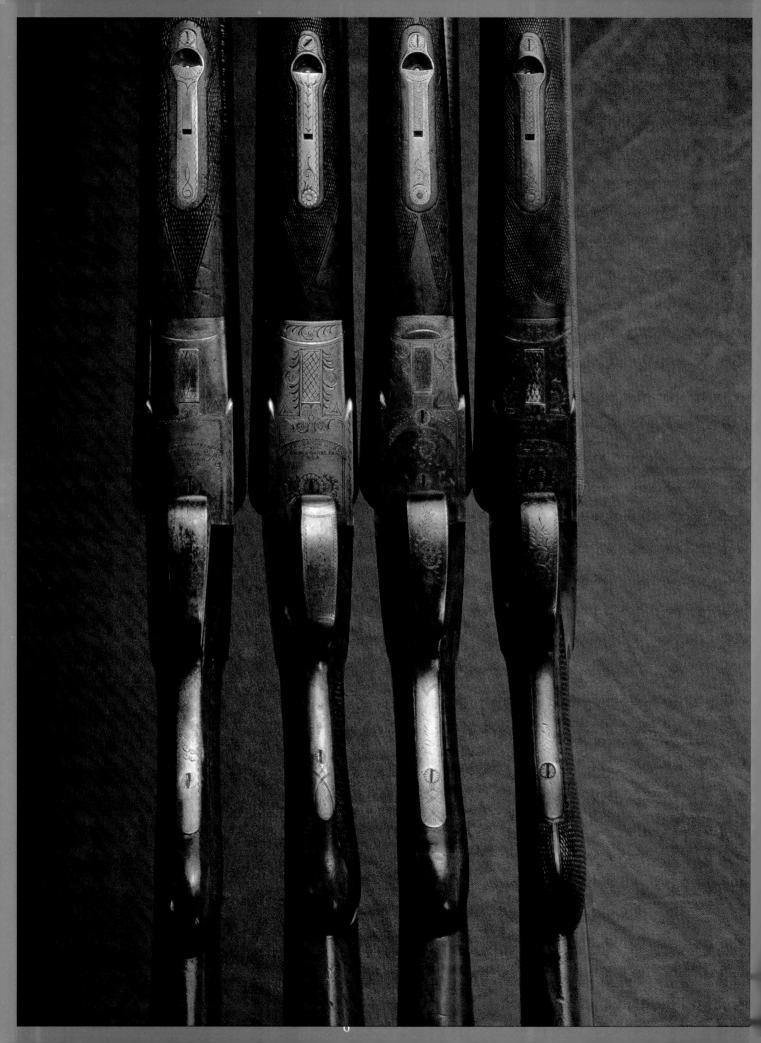

of the main building and fitted up with a target frame
upon which a sheet of white
paper is hung. After a shot is
fired the number of the gun
is written upon it and also
the barrel, either right or left,
is marked upon it, the number of shot holes counted and
if the quantity agrees with
the class desired it goes to
the finisher. The gun tester
was at work and when the
target sheet was brought to
him by a boy, he handed it to
the superintendent with the
remark, 'Eley's gun, right
barrel.'

"'Tom Eley came down
the other day and wanted to

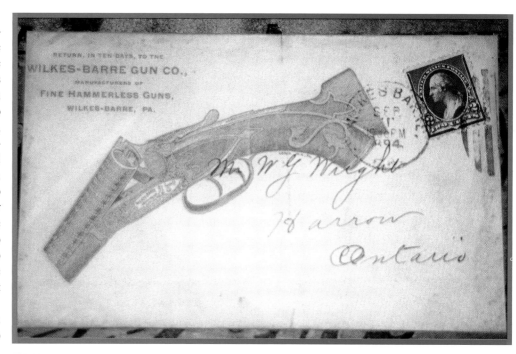

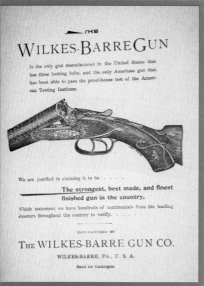

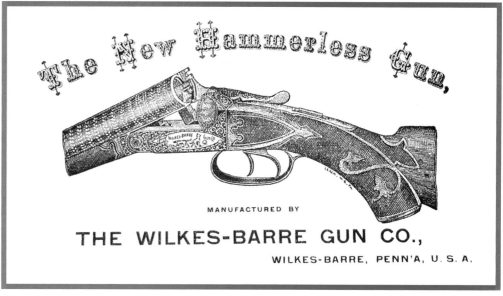

*An 1895 Wilkes-Barre
Gun Company ad.
At right, from top: The enve-
lope enclosure for the pocket
catalogue of 1894—front
and rear cover picture.
On facing page, pictured
from left: Wilkes-Barre
Grades A, B, C, and D.*

know if we could make him a
gun,' said Mr. Collins, 'and of
course he knew just what he
wanted, and you can see
what chance a bird has of
getting away from Tom when
within his range.'

"The paper was so nicely
peppered with little holes
that the reporter modestly

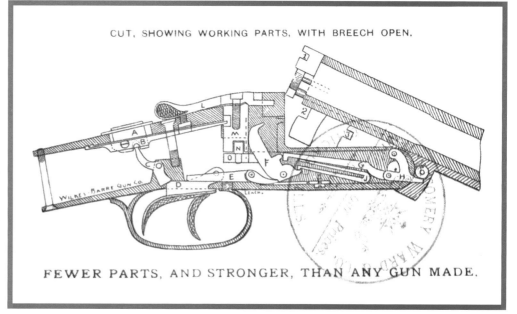

requested a copy, and—flash! bang! the copy of just what Tom's new gun will do can be seen now at the Record office.

"'Yes, there is always a difference made in the barrels of a gun. The second barrel is generally held in reserve for birds that are missed at the first fire, and, of course, is fired at different range.

"'Shotgun making is a comparatively infant industry in America and it is within the last 10 years that American mechanics applied their inventive powers to the making of guns by machinery.

"'Sportsmen's guns were made in this country before that time by certain old makers, but the methods of British and European makers were simply transplanted in this country. We now make everything by machinery excepting the barrels, which we import from Belgium and England. We can buy them much cheaper than we can make them in this country and although I am a democrat, I am grateful to McKinley for protecting this industry.'

"'But is the tariff a tax in this case?'

"'No, it is not. The fact is we are making as good guns in this country as can be made anywhere, and they

do not cost as near as much as the imported guns of this class.'

"'How are the public to know that?'

"'By placing an imported gun beside one of our make. There are two tests by which the value of a gun may be known, first its penetrative power, and next the distribution of the shot over a given surface such as the owner of a gun says of its merits. Let the gun do its own talking and then you will be a listener to some purpose. Owners of imported guns may brag of their killing power, but I am here every day and will make it an object worth the while of any man who wants to venture something on the value of his imported gun.

"'No, you are mistaken we do not make a cheap gun. The class we make will compare with the best of them, both as to finish and lasting qualities.

"'A moment ago I told you our guns are made by machinery, and permit me to explain that in fitting up different parts of the gun we use machinery to do many things that formerly were done by hand, but nevertheless each portion is fitted right to the gun of which it is to be a part. You will observe the parts are all numbered at this stage of the work, that indicates that they have been fitted to certain other parts, and this is as near as we will ever come to making guns by machinery. The parts must be finished and fitted by skilled hands. Yes, this machinery is very expensive. The machines must do their work accurately, so that a few rubs of a file will bring it to proper bearings, but once this plant is complete, it costs very little to keep it up. The barrels come to us in pairs, with a hole in them, but, of course, the bore of the gun is the thing that we take care of for upon this feature the reputation of the maker depends, and, therefore, we bore them out to suit our own ideas.'

"In the case hardening department the work of preparing a batch of frames was in progress, and here is added the variegated coloring to be seen on all first class guns.

Wilkes-Barre, Grade A hammerless.
Facing page: A hammer gun in Quality 2.

"'Yes, we are preparing the tools necessary to make the Parry hammerless guns, and will soon be producing them. We will then give employment to more men. We have about 40 men at present, but we can increase this number to 100 without enlarging the works from present dimensions. The hammerless gun will be a higher priced gun than the pattern we are making now. This style of gun you can make at lots of $30 each and upward. Yes, they are equal to any imported gun and that may cost anywhere from $75 to $100.'

"'Where do all the guns go to?'

"'I give that up. I do know that only about 10 percent of the guns sold in this country were made here before the McKinley bill was passed and from my experience I should say that in a short time this percentage will

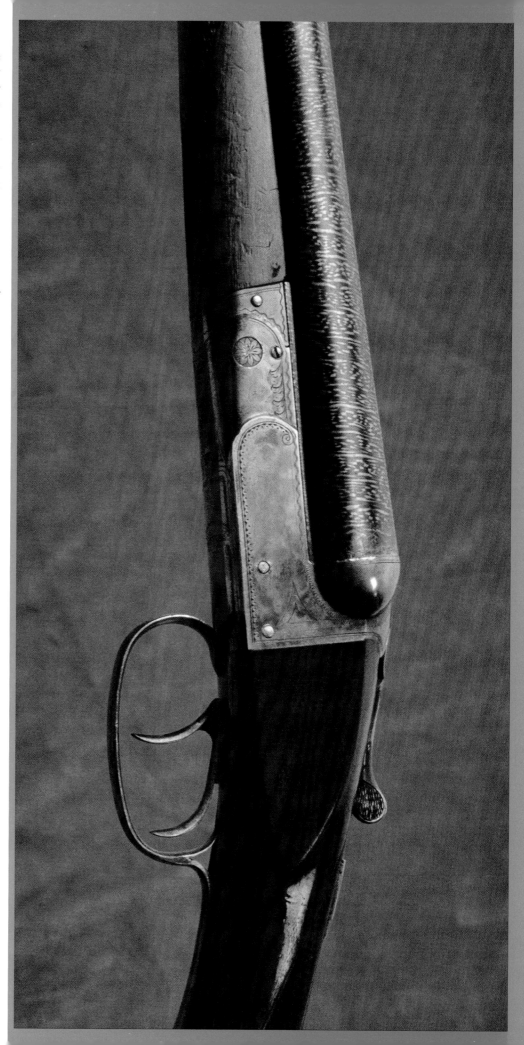

Wilkes-Barre

Ser. No.	Gauge	Grade	Barrel Length	Type	Description
62	12		30		
71	12	B	30	Damascus	Brown gun
78	12	A	30	Twist	Minor scroll and borders
180	12	C	30	Damascus	High condition, name on side
187	12	B		Damascus	Name on side
267	12	B	30	Damascus	
280	12	C	30		Name on side
382	12	C	27	Damascus	Scroll engraved, name on side
428	12	A	30 & 32	Damascus	Poor condition, 2 barrel set, gun won't open, top lever bent A or B Grade, name on side
453	12	B	30	Damascus	High condition, name on side, recoil pad added, bird on the bottom, one screw in bottom
537	12	B	27	Damascus	Scroll engraved, name on bottom, one screw
572	12		30	Damascus	Blued over barrels, name on bottom, flowers on the sides
581	12	B			Frame only, name on bottom
654	12	A			High condition
680	12	A			Name on bottom
688	12	B	30		Name on bottom
690	12	B	30	Damascus	Scroll engraved, name on bottom, restocked, poor fit
729	12	D	30	Damascus	Very good condition, one duck on one side, one woodcock on the other, scroll on the bottom
733	12	A	30	Twist	High condition
768	12	B			Name on bottom
774	12	B	30	Damascus	Good condition, capped pistol grip
775	12	B	30	Damascus	
777	12	A	28	Damascus	Light engraving, name on bottom, one screw
783					
829		A			Brown gun
857	12		30	Twist	Light engraving, name on bottom, one screw
898	12	A	30	Twist	Minor scroll and borders, name on bottom of frame
917	12	B	28	Damascus	Very good condition
983	12	C	28	Damascus	Pistol grip, woodcock and bobwhite, name on bottom, one screw
984	12	C		Damascus	Duck on left and grouse on right, straight grip, old pad, diag. line on side
993	12	B	28	Damascus	One Screw
994	12	C	30	Damascus	Game scene, straight grip
1013	12	B	30	Damascus	80% case, straight grip
1018		D			This gun is from a testimonial so it may not exist, delivered to buyer Mar. 19, 1894
1028	12	D	28	Damascus	One duck and one woodcock
1088					On Antique arms
1097	12	B			
1102	12	A	30	Twist	Barrels only
1113	12	A	30	Twist	Sold on Auction Arms
1128	12	A			Lots of case color
1161	12	D	30	Damascus	Name on bottom, one dog on each side, dog's head on the bottom, 2 screws
1208	12	D	28	Damascus	Two woodcocks on one side and two ruffed grouse on the other, Nine point buck on the bottom, D Grade marked under the triggerguard
1224	12	D	30	Damascus	Two birds on each side, no grade marking, restocked?
1225	12	D		Damascus	
1227	12	A	28	Twist	
1320	12	B	30	Damascus	Pad added, light scroll
1338	12	B	30	Damascus	New buttstock,, name on bottom of frame
1401	12	C	30	Damascus	Exc. condition, game scenes, duck on one side and woodcock on the other
1428	12		30		
1442	12	D		Damascus	2 quail on right side, 2 ducks on the left side, one dog on the bottom
1445		C		Damascus	Duck on left side and rail bird on the right side
1449	12	D	28	Damascus	Two woodcocks on left, two ducks on right, straight grip, old butt pad.

Wilkes-Barre Hammer Guns

Ser. No.	Gauge	Grade	Barrel Length	Type	Description
586	12	2	30	Damascus	High grade, flowers on side, bird on bottom, tear drop
749	12	1	30	Twist	
1025	12	1	30	Twist	Fair cond., border engraved, orig. buttplate
1053	12	1		Twist	N marked on underside of barrels, Parry buttplate, line engraved
1065			30	Twist	
1102			28	Twist	Semi-pistol grip, orig. buttplate
1180	12	1	30	Twist	
1181	12	1	30	Twist	Orig. buttplate, rear rifle sight, refinished wood, brass deer on wood
1202	12	2	30	Twist	
1278	12	1	30	Twist	Orig. buttplate, border engraved, small crack above lock
1319			30	Twist	

Parry Hammer Guns

Ser. No.	Gauge	Grade	Barrel Length	Type	Description
18	12	2	30		Crossbolt and underlug
44	12			Damascus	
46	12	2	32	Laminate	Marked Parry Arms Co., Ithaca, scroll engraving
54		2			Scroll engraved
58	12	2	32		Scroll engraving, replaced hammer
99					Could be 66
142	12	1	30	Twist	Birmingham proof mark on barrels, 243 on triggerguard tang
225					
262	12	1		Twist	High condition
402		1		Twist	Marked Parry Arms Co., Ithaca, NY
425	12	1	30	Twist	
430	12	1	30	Twist	Line and scroll engraved
475			20		Marked Wells Fargo Co. on the buttstock
514	12	1	28	Twist	
515	12	1		Twist	Line engraved

Wilkes-Barre, Grade B

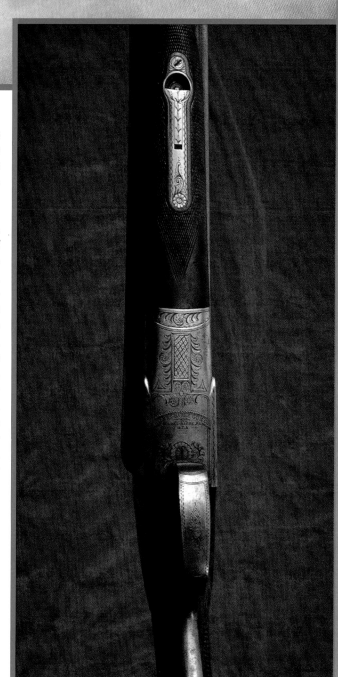

be the other way as all the gun works in the United States have all they can do and all are either increasing their plants or are planning to increase them. One house has taken all the guns we have been able to make so far, but we will put a man of our own on the road this present year. We expect to make 2000.'"

From this close parallel to today's "infomercials" (or even an investment prospectus), one can conclude that by the late winter of 1892, the shotgun manufacturing in Wilkes-Barre was up and running. In effect, the Parry Fire Arms Company of Ithaca, New York, had crossed state lines for, one can only assume to have been, advantageous (and probably pressing) financial reasons. The situation is somewhat similar to George Pratt Foster's avoiding creditors by moving his operation in Taunton, Massachusetts, in the 1850s to Bristol, Rhode Island, and renaming it the Bristol Fire Arm Company. The next salient point is that the company is producing the Parry sidelock hammer double with tooling being prepared to produce the Parry hammerless double. One also notes the obvious "pitch" for custom gun service with the company dealing directly with the client. One also can not fail to notice the subtle "pitch" for investment capital— a great product future thanks to the McKinley tariff guaranteeing an almost sure market. Events over the next few years would drastically alter that rosy picture.

What is also noteworthy in the declamation of the glib Mr. Collins is the absence of any reference to patent holder Edward George Parry. No mention is made of Joseph Tonks or Albert J. Aubrey. They obviously had not yet entered the picture. One also wonders just how many Parry guns bearing the Parry name were produced in Ithaca and how many were produced in Wilkes-Barre.

This article will continue in our Winter 2003 issue.

Small Bores On The Rice Meadow

*Written and Photographed
by Kevin McCormack*

Quality N.

Price: $80.00

Quality G. H.

Fine Damascus Steel Barrels, Fine Figured
American or Imported Stock, Checked and Engraved, Straight or
Pistol Grip, Hard Rubber Butt Plate; No. 14, 14, 16, 20 or 28 Gauge.

MENU

Second Annual Banquet
Of the Shelter Island Gun Club
January 1, 1900

I had just put the tractor back in the garage when the phone rang. It was Ken Camp calling from South Jersey.

"Well," he began, "you're in luck. I can take you and your brother for both days, Wednesday and Thursday. Can't guarantee anything, but there's a few birds on the meadow. Won't be as many or other kinds as there will later in the year, but like I said, I'm booked solid so far except for opening day and this Wednesday and Thursday. I may have somebody cancel later in the season, but not likely. Most of these guys have been with me for 25 or 30 years, and unless one of them dies or quits, you don't have much of an opportunity." I told him we were good for both days. "Great," he said, "be at the landing at 10:30. The tide tops out at noon, so you want to be in amongst 'em as it's making flood. Once it crests, they can sense it and won't jump as good. And once it starts to fall out, they quit for good. We'll take two boats—Jack'll push one of you and I'll take the other. On Thursday, we can switch. So I'll see you at the landing at 10:30. Drive safe."

I hung the phone up. Out on the back porch, I sat down and looked out across my freshly mown lawn. Labor Day weekend, the traditional end of summer. As dusk approached it reminded me that summer, like this splendid day, was waning. Where had it gone? It seemed like an eternity since I'd been afield with a gun in my hands.

Labor Day traditionally marks the opening of dove season in my home state of Virginia, followed by the September 1 opening in neighboring Maryland where I also hunt. I had always considered dove as the singular opening quarry that defined my bird hunting season, and I seldom miss an opportunity to hunt one or the other state's opener. Predictably, the first few days are great. The pace is furious, there are lots of birds, and the shots are challenging. But after those first days the birds get educated, the flights are less predictable, the opportunities for shots are much fewer and farther between, and the afternoons seem too long and too hot to linger in the field. There are these few good days on dove, then the late September "doldrums" until woodcock, quail, and grouse come in. But not this year. This year, we're going rail-birding first.

We would be hunting in every sense of the word, using

Ken Camp has pushed for rail for over 50 years.

boats, guns, and methods that have changed little in design and none in purpose since just after the Civil War. Pole-pushing tiny skiffs through freshwater stands of wild rice, we'd be trying to find, flush, shoot, and retrieve sora rail: birds that would rather run than flush, fly sometimes like a bat and other times like a playing card tossed into a hat, and call like tree frogs peeping when alarmed. And they are scarcely the size of a robin. All told, not your usual gamebird. The first time I went gunning for rail I asked my mentor, a wonderful character steeped in the true lore of the sport, how I should prepare for the trip. What gun should I bring; what shells should I shoot; what should I wear; how should I practice? His answers were simple. "Bring a gun you can go overboard with. I know you like those little Parkers and other double-barrel "popguns," so if you have one you don't mind "dunking," by all means use it. And remember: when you're out after rail, no choke is too open and no shot size is too small." As for the proper wardrobe: "Wear clothes you'd wash your dog in." For practice, he recommended, "You might try balancing on a seesaw and shooting some claybirds off a hand trap—have 'em throw them real close to you." I thanked him, thought about it awhile, and looked off in the distance for a long time. I wasn't real sure I was ready for this. Once we were on the river, however, everything he said would ring true.

On the drive over to South Jersey from our homes outside suburban Washington, Tom and I talked about our upcoming adventure. Small-bore devotees, my brother and I chose guns we felt comfortable with. His was a VH-Grade Parker 28 gauge, bored cylinder and modified. Mine was a .410 gauge Marlin Model 90, bored skeet and skeet. We both shot standard skeet loads of No. 9 shot, only because we couldn't find No. 10, 11, or 12 shot. (One of my treasures is a factory-loaded 12-gauge Western shell marked 2 drams equivalent; 2 ounces of No. 10 shot. Ken told me lots of the old timers shot them in cut-off or skeet bored, light-frame 12 gauges. "The patterns looked like tobacco seed when they hit the water. They sounded like they barely had enough powder to get the charge out of the barrel, but they killed rail-birds!")

We got to Ken's riverfront farm around ten o'clock, and

took the sandy road between his house and the farm-produce stand leading down to the banks of the Maurice River. Huge pumpkins, assorted squashes, and green watermelons lay in the fields on either side of the landing road. Tall stands of sunflowers swayed gently in the late morning ble-ended rowboats with not quite enough freeboard. Pulled up on the bank and examined closely, they exhibited the unmistakable characteristics of true genius in nautical engineering. Like so many other specialized watercraft, they are incomparable when suited to their designated task,

Ungainly on shore, rail-bird skiffs are marvels of nautical engineering,
and become delicately balanced shooting platforms once waterborne.

breeze, and small flocks of dove cruised gently over them, looking for an early snack. At the end of the sandy road lay our boats. Viewed afloat in shallow water at the landing, the boats gave little more impression than that of narrow, dou- and virtually worthless for anything else. The first thing you notice is the graceful sheer of the gunwales and the manner in which the design is carried from stem to stern. The generous cockpit coaming, just high enough for protection while paddling to the gunning grounds if the winds get "frisky," gives a great sense of self-assurance. And the flair of the hull, designed to splay the head-high stalks of wild rice to either side while not breaking or crushing them, affords you a clear shot when your mark "jumps." Lastly, the curve, or "rocker," built into the bottom of the hull aligned along the keel, allows the seasoned gunner to apply some "body English" to help his pusher shove off when the skiff high-centers or "hangs" on a marsh stump or the remnants of an old muskrat house. Moving fore and aft in syncopated rhythm, you time your "lunges" to the pusher's thrusts on the pole, and "sleighride" down the low side of the hummock by counterbalancing the bow. Once established, the pusher and gunner's motions working in unison produce a barely noticeable hesitation as the flat-bottomed skiff slides through the marsh. Balancing yourself in a shooting position in a rail-bird skiff being poled through a wild rice meadow is much like my mentor described it: like seesawing back and forth on a teeterboard while your quarry flushes in front, beside, ahead of, and (occasionally) behind you. But it's also like learning to ride a bicycle: once you've got it down, you never forget it.

Ken and our other pusher, Jack Smith, arrived as we were examining the boats. After short introductions and a basic "rail-birder's safety course," we stowed our gear, pushed off, and headed northeast into the Maurice River. Dressed like the needy, we cut quite a figure paddling upriver to the wild rice stands. When we got there the paddles were stowed, Ken and Jack manned the poles, told us to stand up and find our toe holds, and gave the word to load up and get ready. "They could be anywhere," Jack said. "So be ready—all set?"

"Yes!" said Tom. "Let's go!" Jack gave a hearty thrust on the pole, and Tom hit the deck.

"Whoa!" Jack yelled. "Ya got ta get yer sea legs yet! Make sure you got yer front toe hooked under the rail." (The "rail" is the one- by two-inch piece of lumber or 1¼ inch closet pole set just under the front seat, set to hook your forward foot as you get under way.) Jack politely continued, "Keep your knees slightly bent and your gun between your hands, if you know what I mean. That way, if you fall, you'll fall to the side or straight back, like you did. That's good, 'cause that way, you won't tear any tendons or pop any ligaments like you would if you pitched forward with your knees locked. And holding your gun like you did helps you keep your balance, sorta like a high-wire walker uses his balancing pole, ya know? Gotta stay loose and move with the boat!"

"Yeah," Tom replied warily, "they're a little more lively than they look!"

We poled off together, skiffs about 20 yards apart, running a slight zig-zag pattern through the meadow. The wild rice stands, some standing well over our heads, held an amazing diversity of life. Red-winged blackbirds, killdeer,

Tom McCormack goes to the "ready" position with his Parker 28-gauge

and plover twittered about. Occasionally, knots of teal would explode from secluded ponds barely bigger than a bathtub, and now and then the odd widgeon or pintail would rocket out of a meandering creek, barely wide enough to merit a thought as to what might be hidden upstream. Suddenly, Ken's voice boomed from astern: "Mark right! Mark *Right!*

as he and pusher Jack Smith enter a thick and luxuriant rice meadow on the Maurice River near Port Elizabeth, New Jersey.

Mark Your Other Right!" Low and away, a rail-bird fluttered mantis-like out from under our right gunwale, barely a foot off the water and "threading" the rice stalks like a needle. I fired twice and missed. "Got to get right on 'em, stay right down their backs, that's all there is to it," said Ken. In the next ten minutes, I missed two more. I commented that my

over/under .410 might be a "high shooter." Ken replied, "Well, then, put it right on their back ends and *hold* it there; don't lead over them. Most people miss by giving them too much of everything: too high, too low, too fore, too aft. Stay *on* 'em!" Fifteen minutes later, one spun away from amidships, going straight away at a 90-degree angle, but rising

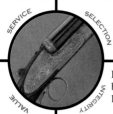

rapidly in that crazy, broken-wing flight that they effect. This time, I stayed "*on* 'em!" The bird collapsed in a shower of feathers. After that, I connected. Meanwhile, Tom was having my same problem. Jack admonished him, "Do like your brother and stay with 'em. Don't want to have to chase any down to Cape May!" Moments later, one sprang literally from underneath the stem of their skiff, careening like a butterfly. The bird barely made it five feet from the bow before Tom's little 28-gauge Parker barked. When he shot, a geyser of water the size of a trash-can lid bracketed the

skeet loads of No. 9s. In his 1952 book, *Duck Boats, Blinds, Decoys and Eastern Seaboard Wildfowling,* Raymond R. Camp outlined the way to go in selecting the proper load for rail-birding, "For years most rail-shooters have sworn by what they considered to be the standard rail-load of seven-eighths of an ounce of No. 11 shot backed up by the equivalent of two drams of powder. This load is claimed by the ballisticians to be equally effective in the twenty- and twelve-gauge shell. This is not a standard load, and it is necessary to pay twenty dollars more a thousand to have it

This 1909 vintage Parker 28-gauge fills the bill for rail-bird shooting.

bird. Jack allowed smugly, "I think you got him. Right yonder out front he is, dead on the widder."

The rest of our "push" went well. We saw relatively few birds, but managed to bag seven. Our two and a half-hour tide came and went all too fast. "Don't feel bad," said Ken. "You guys really aren't used to it yet, and the birds aren't here in near the numbers we'll see later. I must admit, though, once you got settled down, you guys were pretty fair shots. We'll have more chances tomorrow."

Back at the motel later that evening, we relived the day's hunt. By and large, we both agreed that our choice of guns was correct, and that by using them within their intended limits, they made fine rail-bird guns. I've had a long-time fascination with using small-bore guns for the smaller species of gamebirds and to me, the open-bored 28-gauge just seems "right" for rail. The birds are a lot like dove; it doesn't take much to bring one down, so powerful loads and big shot aren't necessary. The commercial loads available in 28-gauge nowadays are pretty much restricted to high-velocity field loads of No. 6 or No. 7½ shot or standard

loaded, but it is worthwhile, for in the proper gun it throws a good pattern and kills the rail cleanly with little damage to the flesh. If this load can not be obtained a regular skeet-load will give the next-best results." Today, I'd give a lot to spend that extra twenty bucks for a thousand-round run of No. 11s!

The Parker Brothers Order Book record for Tom's gun shows SN 151456 as one of seven 28-gauge "Vulcan PG Hmls." The Vulcan pistol grip, hammerless grades which were requested on order number 125480, were received from the Simmons Hardware Company of St. Louis on September 20, 1909, and shipped to them on November 6 of that year. Of the seven guns on the order, three had 26-inch barrels and four had 28-inch barrels. This gun is the only one of the lot that shows a notation in the order for choke boring: right barrel cylinder; left barrel modified. The price at the time was fifty dollars per gun, and during the heydey of small-bore production (roughly 1908–1915), Parker built a lot of them. Predictably, most of them were ordered with short barrels and very open chokes (the 26-inch, cylinder and modified combination was very popular,

and the Parker Brothers Record Books are full of them), but occasionally you'll come across a 30- or a 32-inch gun, which is relatively rare. (Contrary to popular misconception, Parker guns in 28 gauge are not rare in the truest sense of the word; Parker introduced them as early as 1899 and after the Remington buyout in 1934, they were offered right up until the end of Parker production in 1947.)

My little gun, a Marlin Model 90 .410 over and under, SN 1736, was made sometime between 1950 and 1958 (my gun has a side rib separating the barrels; M 90s made prior to 1950 had vent-separated barrels). Another interesting feature of this little gun is that it has double triggers, an unusual feature on an over and under. Luckily, I'd shot the little gun enough so that I was accustomed to using them, and had no problems with either them or the safety "in between" shots. As far as the .410 goes as a choice of gun for "serious" hunting, I'm well aware of the widely held disdain most gun writers harbor for the little gun, "in all but expert hands." I'm no expert, but I once did kill a limit of woodcock (five at the time) in less than an hour over a friend's good Brittany using a nifty little L.C. Smith .410. Keenly aware of the ribbing I knew I'd get later about it, I kept good notes: I fired 12 shells of three-inch No. 7$^{1}/_{2}$ shot to bag my birds, and I don't recall having to shoot any of them twice. And, sure, I missed some clean! But I was careful not to overextend the gun. My operating theory in using the .410 for hunting is that if the little gun can powder a target into confetti at the middle station on a skeet field (roughly 22 yards), then the gauge can successfully be used to kill small, relatively fragile, thin-skinned game birds at that range and under. Rail-bird hunting fits all these parameters in terms of choosing an adequate weapon: a somewhat fragile target taken at very close range using extremely small shot. Like anything else, if you practice, it works; thus the .410 remains a favorite of mine for rail shooting. Others seem to think so, too. Outdoor writer Worth Mathewson, after a rail-bird hunt on Maryland's Patuxent River, wrote, "We had two guns on the marsh. Myself in Glenn's boat and a fellow who had bid for a rail-bird day...at a Ducks Unlimited dinner in Jim Owings' boat. He was using a borrowed 28 bore while I was using a 20. I feverishly wished I had had a side-by-side .410. I think this situation would have offered one of the very few valid opportunities to use this bore in the field."

The next day, our hunt was even better. Although we bagged only a few more birds, the weather was cooler and the wind was not as strong, making the paddle to and from the meadows much like a lazy Sunday afternoon canoe ride. And our "sea legs" were better, we shot straighter, and, most of all, our guides seemed to genuinely enjoy our company. On the way back in, I asked Ken why they called the wild rice stands "meadows." He responded with a fascinating story: "Well, years ago, a lot of this marsh we've been gunning on, you could walk on back then. There were lots of areas that were diked against the river that people used to graze livestock on and cut salt hay off of. But that's all a long time ago, now. Kind of made me smile, thinking back, while we were down on the lower meadow this morning. Know where your brother made that real nice shot on the sliding bird, then you killed two, then missed a third while you were reloading? Well, that's where I learned to drive a car, right down there in that meadow. I remember my dad teaching me to steer and work the gas and the clutch, same as he taught me how to pole a skiff. After the war, a lot of the farms went down and people let the dikes go, the river came back in and created that beautiful marsh down there. Yeah, there's lots of my fondest memories down there on the rice meadows." As we drifted along, I watched the droplets from Ken's paddle poke ringlets in the placid surface and thought...my fondest memories...mine too, Ken, mine too.

Author's notes and acknowledgements: Many thanks to our rail-bird guides and "pole-pushers," Ken Camp and Jack Smith, of Port Elizabeth, New Jersey. Similar appreciation is in order to Frank Astemborski of Delanco, New Jersey, and Jim Owings of Potomac, Maryland, both of whom provided important anecdotal and technical information on the people, culture, and sport of rail-birding.

*Marlin Model 90 .410 O/U proved a good choice for rail. Very rare No. 12 shot loads;
sizes 10, 11, and 12 were the choice of experienced rail-bird shooters in the "old days."
Below: Elusive quarry brought to bag—using vintage 20-gauge loads of No. 11 shot.*

Quality Guns...

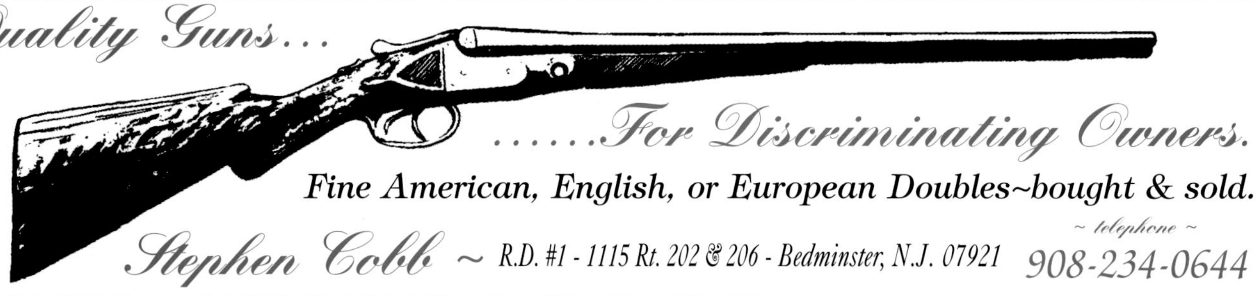

......For Discriminating Owners.

Fine American, English, or European Doubles~bought & sold.

Stephen Cobb ~ *R.D. #1 - 1115 Rt. 202 & 206 - Bedminster, N.J. 07921*

~ *telephone* ~
908-234-0644

12 GAUGE GUNS

HOLLAND & HOLLAND - Dominion sidelock ejector, 30" bls., IC/M, CC 100% blue 100%, wood 100%, refinished, 14-3/4" LOP, drop 1-3/16"x2-3/16", cast off 1/4", 6 pounds 9 ounces, checkered butt........................**$5,900**

WEBLEY & SCOTT - Matched pair of Model 700 game guns, 28" bls., IC/IM (.010/.030), wt. 6 lbs. 7 ozs., straight stock, double triggers, cased in two gun leather hard case. Guns are in 99% condition **$5,500**

ARMY & NAVY C.S.L. - Double rifle, 12 bore, 26" Damascus barrels, fully rifled, back action hammer gun, 3 leaf sight **$7,500**

LINSLEY BROS. - Boxlock nonejector, 26" bls. choked .000/.015, 2-1/2" chambers, LOP 14" to wood. Churchill rib, 6-1/4 lbs., DT. , CC 30%, cased............................**$2,600**

JOSEPH LANG & SON - Boxlock ejector, 2" *chambers*, 28" bls. M/F, 13-7/8" LOP over pad, ST, DT, bls. reblued. 5 lbs. 14 ozs. **$3,500**

JOSEPH LANG & SON - SLE, key detachable locks, 27" bls. Skt. (0.005)/IC (.010), recondition 100%, single nonselective trigger, 14" LOP from single trigger, four gold inlaid dogs on case colored action. Weight 6-3/4 lbs. Drop 1-3/4" x 2-3/4". Cased..**$7000**

STEPHEN GRANT & SONS - Sidelock ejector, 29" bls. IM (.030) and F (.040), Miller SST, border engraved, straight stock, wt. 7 lbs. 4 ozs., fine English sidelock...........**$5,000**

JAMES WOODWARD & SONS - SLE, sidelock 28" M/M, DT, st. stock, LOP 14-1/2" over pad, rebarreled by W. Richards..**$10,000**

E.J. CHURCHILL - BLE, "Hercules" Best Grade boxlock, scalloped action, self opener, 25" bls............, IC/IC, butt stock is of cross over style. Made to shoot from right shoulder but positioning in front of left eye. Blue wear on bls. from use in scabbard **$2,950**

D.B. CROCKART - (Scottish) sidelock ejector gun, 30" IC/Full, DT, CC 50% LOP 13-3/4" over buttplate. **$1,500**

J. DICKSON & SON - Edinburgh, boxlock, extractors, 30" M/F, DT, PG stock, triggerguard tang extends to grip cap, LOP 14-1/4" over pad. Case colors 95%, Wt. 7 lbs. 15 ozs. 1-3/8 oz. proof, excellent clays or waterfowl. **$3,600**

MIDLAND GUN CO. - Birmingham, boxlock SxS, 30" Full/Full. In like new condition, str. stock, splinter FE. .**$2,500**

MIDLAND GUN CO. - Birmingham, back action sidelock hammer gun, round body. 30" bls. Cyl/Full. 6 lbs. 12 ozs.........**$1,500**

A. FRANCOTTE - 14E boxlock, 28" IC/M, DT, half pistol, CC 50-60%, good shooting dimensions, excellent gun.......**$2,900**

A. FRANCOTTE - Sidelock, ejector, 28-1/2" bls., IC/M, LOP 14", chambers 2-1/2" straight stock, double triggers, splinter forend, case colors 100%, engraved with stags and dogs. Cased **$8,500**

A. FRANCOTTE - Sidelock action, 28% reblued barrels, Cyl/IC, straight stock, LOP 14-1/4" over solid pad, CC 20%, bushed pins hidden third fastener, rose and scroll engraved, weight 6 lbs. 6 ozs..................................**$4,900**

GEBR. ADAMY - Suhl, Germany, BLE, O/U 30" bls. IC/M, DT, solid rib, LOP 14-5/8" over pad, game scene engraved **$2,900**

FERLIB - SLE, 26" IC/M, coin rec., light scroll engraving, DT, gold line accents, new. **$5,000**

DUMOULIN - SLE, rounded body, 27-1/2" bls. Cyl (.002) & Mod (,020) SST, CC 100% Blue 100%, wood 99%, weight 6 lbs. 11 ozs., hidden third fastener, bushed pins, LOP 14-3/16" over pad **$4,800**

DUMOULIN - BLE, scalloped action, sideclips, tear drops, 27-1/2" bls., F/F, DT, CC 100%. Blueing 98%, wood 99%. Wt. 6 lbs. Hidden third fastener. **$2,800**

DE BRAUWER A GAND - SLE, 29-3/4" bls., cyl/full, bushed pins, articulated trigger, st. stock, LOP 15-1/8" over pad and spacer. 13-7/8" to end of wood. This Belgian gun is as good as a Purdey, but can be purchased for half the price. **$6,400**

L.C. SMITH - Ideal Grade, featherweight action, 30" IC/Full, bl blue thin, CC 50%, needs grip cap, 14-1/4"x1-5/8"x2-5/16"..**$1,175**

L.C. SMITH - Trap Grade, Long Range, 32" Full/Full, 3" chambers, straight stock, SST, CC 98%, blue 98%. This is a very rare collector's gun that handles well in the field**$4,500**

PARKER - Trojan, 28" bls. M/F, CC 50%, very nice clean Trojan, No. 2 frame, no dents or dings................**$1,500**

PARKER - VHE, 2 barrels, 26" Skt/Full and 28" Skt/Full, 2 forends,single selective triggers, PG, in Browning case ..**$3,400**

PARKER - VH, 28" M/F, pistol grip, double triggers, action and bls. and wood redone. Pach. pad, No. 2 frame **$950**

PARKER - DH, 32" F/F, pistol grip, CC 10%, 14-1/2"x1-5/8"x2-1/2", 2-5/8" cham. **$3,700**

PERAZZI - MX8 B, 2 bls., 29-1/2" full on top/choke tubed on bottom, 2nd set 26-3/4" with "Teague" choke tubes. All in near new condition. Excellent trap skeet or sporting combination..**$5,700**

BROWNING - Superposed, Ser. No. 25XX, twin single trigger, Diana Grade, 2nd year of production, very rare gun. Wood refinished. Metal is in excellent condition. Chokes have been opened from F/F to IC Mod ..**$4,500**

WINCHESTER - Model 12-Y, Super Pigeon, 30" vent rib, full choke, No. 5 engraved, B carved wood, 98% condition .**$2,800**

WINCHESTER - Model 101 Trap, Diamond Grade, 30" step rib, top bl. full. Bottom Winchoked (4 tubes). As new in hard case **$1,750**

ITHACA - NID, SxS, 26" bls., Skt/Mod. Near new cond. **$1,400**

A.H. FOX - Grade A, 28" M/F, LOP 14-1/4", drop 1-3/4"x3", 6 lbs. 13 oz., blue 95%, top lever right of center **$1,600**

A.H. FOX - Sterlingworth, 28" bls. IC/Full, well used but still very servicable. PG stock 14-3/16"x1-3/16"x2-13/16" **$695**

W.W. GREENER - Single barrel trap, 32" full choke, vent rib, ejector, half pistol grip, ebony forend tip, LOP 14-1/2" over solid leather faced pad, game scene engraved...**$2,800**

20 GAUGE GUNS

FRANCOTTE - Sideplate deluxe, 26" chopper lump barrels, Mod/Full, 14-3/8", single trigger, side clips, game scene engraving with raised gold inlays. Gun is 99.9%. In Brady case **$10,500**

DARNE - R 10, sliding breech, case colors 100%, 25-1/2" barrels, choke Skeet/Modified, LOP 14-3/8"..............**$2,200**

PARKER BROS. - GHE, 26" bls. Cyl/Cyl, CC 25% bl. Blue and wood 99%, has Miller single trigger.................**$4,000**

A.H. FOX - Sterlingworth 28" M/F, LOP 13-11/16"x1-5/8"x3", lever well right of center, CC 50%, blue 99%, 5 lbs. 11 oz., 2-1/2" chambers...**$2,000**

ITHACA - Flues, Field, 26" Mod/Full, beavertail forend, PG, no CC, action is tight **$650**

B. RIZZINI - "Artemis," 28" bls. choke tubed, coin receiver with birds & scroll, very pretty wood, straight stock. Near new condition. **$1,700**

B. RIZZINI/SIG SAUER - Aurora, "L.L. Bean New Englander," 28" O/U, choke tubes, CC receiver, new and unfired, in aluminum hard case **$1,875**

BERETTA - Side by side, coin rec., 26" bls., IC/Mod, 6 lbs. 1 oz., LOP 13-1/2" over pad, some patina on outside of bls. ST **$1,200**

THOMAS BLAND - SxS boxlock with ejectors, 28" bls. Mod/Mod, CC 95%, 5 lbs. 6 ozs...........................**$3,400**

FRANCHI - O/U, 27" bls., IC/Mod, 6 lbs., excellent condition...**$675**

PERAZZI - MX20, 27-1/2" bls., IC/M, SST, nice wood, near new condition **$5,700**

28 GAUGE GUNS

HOLLAND & HOLLAND - Back action sidelock, round body hammer gun, 26" barrels, Full/Imp.Mod, 2-1/2" cham., bls. reblued...**$5,900**

PERAZZI - MX28, 29-1/2" bls. M/F, LOP 14-3/4". As new condition, cased......................................**$12,000**

WINCHESTER/PARKER REPRO - DHE, two barrel set. 26" IC/M, 28" rechoked to Skt/Skt. Straight stock, LOP 14-3/4", beavertail forend, in 2 barrel case with canvas cover. Near new cond...........................**$4,400**

ITHACA - Flues Model, Grade I, 26" bls. Cyl/IC, action light patina, DT..**$2,700**

WESTLEY RICHARDS - BLNE, 27" Cyl/Cyl, reblued, LOP 13-7/8 over pad, weight 4 lbs. 11 ozs., in proof at 2-3/4". CC 100% (rehardened)..............................**$4,900**

ZANOTTI - SxS scalloped action boxlock, CC 90%, straight stock, ST, 25" barrels IC/M **$4,200**

J. BLANCH - BLNE, 27-1/4" nitro proof Damascus bls. 2-3/4", IC/LT. Mod, 14-5/8" LOP, very nice London boxlock **$3,800**

.410 GAUGE GUNS

ZOLI/RIZZINI - "Abercrombie & Fitch" side x side, 26" bls. Mod/Full, case colors 98%, blue 99%, semi-pistol grip, semi-beavertail forend, double triggers,, extractors, 5 lbs. 3 oz. **$3,000**

W. DARLOW - Belgium made SxS, 28" bls., Cyl/Full, DT, straight stock, extractors, 4 lbs. 13 ozs. **$1,375**

B. HALLIDAY - BLNE, 2-1/2" chambers, 27" barrels, Cyl/Mod (.000/.013), DT, str. stock **$2,500**

ENGLISH MADE - No maker's name, SxS hammer 410, 30" steel barrels Nitro proofs, Full/Full, DT **$2,000**

PATSTONE - Back action round body sidelock hammer gun, 26" bls. Cyl/Mod, 2-1/2" chambers, straight stock, LOP 13-3/4"..**$2,100**

RIFLES

J.P. SAUER & SOHN - Double rifle, cal. 303 British, one standing and one folding sight plus folding peep sight, steel grip cap, bullet trap, set triggers, scalloped action boxlock with crossbolt, new condition **$9,800**

JOHN RIGBY - Double rifle, cal. 470. 3-1/4" Nitro Express, 3 leaf express sights, metal grip cap, leather covered pad **$16,000**

FRANCOTTE - Double rifle, Cal. 7x57 R, 24" barrels, standing V notch sight plus claw mounted Kahles scope, bushed pins, hidden third fastener, case colors 98%. blue 100%...**$9,500**

ARMY & NAVY C.S.L. - Double rifle, 12 bore, fully rifled 26" Damascus barrels, 3 leaf 100-200-300 yd. sights. Back action hammer gun. Believed to be made by Manton. Weighs 10 lbs.1 oz. Very nice condition. **$7,500**

JAMES PURDEY & SONS - Double rifle, underlever hammer, cal. .450 BP, 3-1/4" case, 75% CC, reblue 95% **$14,000**

FRANZ SODIA - Double rifle, cal. .458 Win. Mag., ejectors, 26" bls., double triggers, coin finish rec. with 7 gold inlays. Cased.......................................**$25,000**

RUGER - Custom, Ruger No. 1 rifle, fantastic wood, custom octagon 25" barrels with gold bands at muzzle and breech steel grip cap, Pachmayr Old English rifle pad. Engraved by "Gino, C" left side leopard with charging buffalo right side is tiger eating plains game carcass. Surrounded by very fine scroll. Quarter rib scope block with Leupold Vari-X III - 2.5x8. Cased in oak and leather. **$8,000**

GASPARINI - SxS double rifle, boxlock, Cal. 7x65R, 24" bls. Case colored action, new in box....................**$3,950**

SAVAGE - Model 99, .303 cal. 26" barrel, knife blade front sight, Rocky Mountain rear sight, straight stock, metal rifle butt, brass cartridge counter **$350**

GRIFFIN & HOWE - Caliber .375, quarter rib with 2 leaf express sight and Griffin & Howe quick detachable scope mount, checkered steel buttplate and steel grip cap. Rose wood forend tip. Engraved floor plate and scope mounts, Kahles scope **$6,000**

RUGER - 44 Magnum carbine, Cal. 44 mag. Receiver sight, near new...**$450**

BROWNING - BL-22, deluxe 22 cal., SL, LR lever action, tube feed, new in box **$375**

MAUSER - Customized, Cal. 6.5x55, black composite stock with pad, Leupold Vari-X 3x9 scope, Jaeger trigger **$475**

MISCELLANEOUS GUNS

PARKER BROS. - E Grade (GH), 10 ga. 3-1/2" chambers, 32" barrels, believed done by Remington. Around 1940. CC 98% bl. blue and triggerguard 99.5%, LOP 14-7/8" over pad. PG, splinter forend, very rare gun. Also an excellent shooting gun **$5,500**

F. STIRLING - Percussion muzzleloading, 14 ga. Cased in mahogany with full accessories, very good condition .**$2,500**

MERKEL - Action double rifle, Cal. 45-70, game scene engraved, 3 leaf express sights. As new cond..**$6,400**

SEMPERT & KRIEGHOFF - "Trumpf" drilling, 16x16x7.8-57, horn buttplate and triggerguard, pop up rear sight, 23-1/2" bls. **$3,500**

H. BARELLA / J. REIMERS KJOBENHAVN - Drilling, 12/12x5.3MM (22 Hornet), horn triggerguard and buttplate, pistol grip stock with bullet trap for 5 rifle cartridges, claw mount base/no rings. 15-20% case color **$3,800**

Many Hammer Breech-loading Guns. Call For Availability.

I am always in need of good quality firearms. If you have items for sale, I would like to have a chance to purchase. I need new inventory. Consignments accepted.

E-mail me at tarheel07921@yahoo.com

Browning's Best Gun

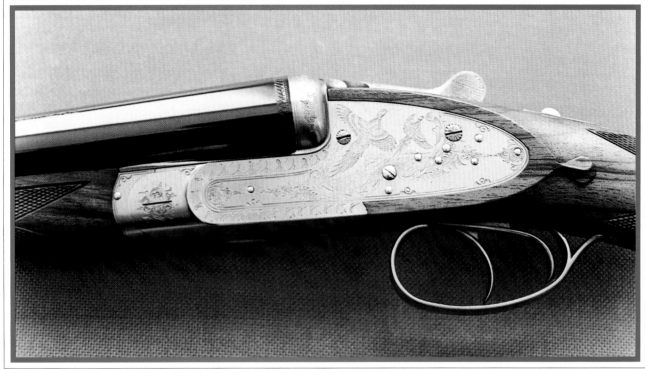

*Written and Photographed
by Colin McLagan*

From 1983 until 1987, Browning made the B-SS side-lock, its best gun. There, it has been said. The blood pressure of a number of readers will no doubt be rising upon reading these words. Some will be apoplectic, and e-mail obscenities. Shortly, my name will be hypenated with "heretic" and I will be blacklisted from membership with the Browning Collectors Association. Cups engraved with my name will be turned upside down in solemn ceremonies… Well, maybe that is a bit exaggerated. However, some owners of Browning over-unders will be ready to vigorously argue the merits of their guns, and rightly so.

In this case, however, I am not using "best" as a comparison with other Browning shotguns. Rather, the term "best" is used in the lexicon of fine English double guns, meaning made to the highest standards and fit for use with driven birds in the company of people whose name often starts with "Lord" or "Lady."

Browning made its B-SS sidelock in small numbers in the 1980s, which has largely remained a best (sorry—couldn't resist) kept secret. It was an inspired effort at making a "best" gun, and it came close (if it did not succeed), even by the exacting standards of critics. The late Don Zutz, for example, wrote several articles nearly a decade ago about sidelocks and game guns in which the B-SS sidelock received warm praise:

"The biggest bargain in a game gun type of smoothbore is Browning's B-SS sidelock. It isn't a perfect replica of the British Best Gun's balance, but it isn't half bad at its advertised price of $1,500. And it is a true sidelock! Browning has had to take into consideration the American penchant for heavy loads and, possibly, steel shot; hence, the barrels have heavier walls than a true game gun. But despite that, the B-SS sidelock has class and han-dling qualities that won't cause a good wingshot to miss many birds. ("The 'Gun' Defined; The 'Game Gun' Featured," *Wing & Shot*, December/ January, 1989–1990.)

In that same article, Zutz excoriates Spanish-made doubles and does not even mention Italian doubles. The popular American-made double classics, such as Winchester Model 21s, L.C. Smiths, Lefevers, Parkers, Ithacas, and Foxes, Zutz relegates to a separate category, "bird gun." Zutz was highly selective about the doubles that were included in the pantheon of British game guns, and it is a testament to the quality and handling characteristics of the B-SS sidelock that Zutz included them in the heady company of Purdeys and other high-end makers.

The B-SS sidelock is a "Holland pattern" gun, which is a polite way of saying it is an imitation of the Holland and Holland sidelock. Spanish-made guns, such as Arrietas and AyAs, are likewise Holland-pattern guns, as are many other well made doubles. A list of the standard features on the B-SS sidelock includes straight English stock, double triggers, selective ejectors, chopper-lump barrels, intercepting sears, cocking indicators, checkered butts, silver-plated triggers, Purdey-style forend release, and coin-finished receivers.

Browning made a total seven hundred and fourteen 12 gauges, and four hundred and fifty 20 gauges. As best as I can determine, the B-SS sidelocks were not made to order, and the only options were 26-inch and 28-inch barrels, and 12 or 20 gauge. The typical dimensions of the B-SS side-locks are $14^1/_4$ inches of pull, $1^1/_2$ inches of drop at the comb, and $2^1/_2$ inches of drop at the heel, with very little or no cast. Two engraving patterns were offered; one was rose and scroll,

Flushing pheasants on lockplate are well illustrated. The drop points are found on game-scene versions only.

the other game scene. Oddly Browning denies that it ever offered the B-SS sidelock with anything other than rose and scroll engraving. The accompanying photographs dispel this notion, and in the course of writing this article, I have had the opportunity to examine several game-scene doubles and speak with dealers who had them for sale, and all were, or sounded to be, identical. I suspect enough time has lapsed since they were made that some of the details have been forgotten. I should add that the game-scene guns are far fewer than the rose and scroll, and that I have never seen nor heard of a 20 gauge with the game-scene engraving. Somewhere some must exist; fortunate are the owners of such light, elegant shotguns. The same should be said for the owners of any of the B-SS sidelocks.

In addition to the different engraving, other distinctions exist between the game-scene and rose and scroll engraved guns. The game-scene guns have drop points, finer checkering with more coverage, higher-grade wood, and a different checkering pattern on the butt. When asked to explain the existence of the game-scene gun, one of Browning's employees alluded to the possibility that an order was placed by a large dealer, such as Griffin & Howe, who then finished the gun to suit its clientele. If this were true, however, it would seem that there would be some evidence of a dealer's name stamped or engraved somewhere on the gun. However, each of the game-scene guns carries the same roll-stamped language on the barrels which is seen on the rose and scroll guns.

On the left barrel:
Browning Arms Company, Morgan, Utah & Montreal P.Q. Made in Japan
On the right barrel:
B-S/S Special Steel 12 Ga. Shells - 2-3/4"
No other reference to the maker or a dealer exists anywhere else on the game-scene gun. On the bottom of the receiver of the rose and scroll engraved gun, the name "Browning" appears.

All of the B-SS sidelocks were made by Miroku in Japan, the same maker who fabricated the B-SS boxlock and who still makes the Citori over-unders. The craftsmen at Miroku obviously benefited from the years of work on Browning's other doubles, for when they were asked to make the B-SS sidelock, they were up to the task. The wood-to-metal fit on the sidelock is superb, and the checkering is flawless. The butt of the rose and scroll gun is unique, with an interesting linear pattern running on angles across the butt. The butt checkering pattern on the game-scene-engraved gun, however, is more restrained, if not conventional. That does not take away from the execution, which is first rate. The

engraving on the rose and scroll engraved guns was acid etched, and then chased out by engravers at Miroku. I am uncertain about the engraving on the game-scene guns since Browning denies their existence. It would make sense that the same process was used. In both cases, the engraving is attractive and contains fine portions associated with the scrollwork, which suggests that Miroku's engravers did more than simply chase the engraving out.

Since Browning was unable to contribute much toward my understanding of the B-SS sidelock, I was forced to discover information from other sources. For example, Buck Hamlin, the dean of American doubles, once worked on a

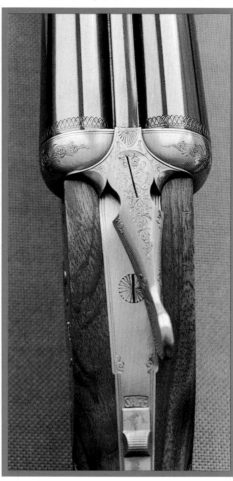

The front page of the Browning B-SS boxlock manual—including sidelock information which was an apparent afterthought.
Top view of game-scene version is without top-rib engraving.

Belgian guild gun which looked exactly like the rose and scroll engraved B-SS sidelock. He surmised that Browning used a Belgian-made double, such as the one in his shop, as the prototype for the B-SS sidelock. This makes sense in light of Browning's Belgian connections. When Buck wrote Browning and inquired about the Belgian gun, he received a non-responsive reply which offered little in the form of an explanation about the origins of the B-SS sidelock.

Kirk Merrington, the English-trained barrel expert, indicated that he had sleeved a number of the B-SS sidelocks. This was not to repair damaged barrels; rather, the owners simply wanted more barrel length. One does not spend the kind of money it takes to sleeve a shotgun, especially if nothing is wrong with the barrels, on just any double. He also mentioned that some of the ranches in Texas stocked the sidelocks for their guests' use. I suppose if a guest shows up with a pump or semi-automatic 12 gauge for a quail hunt, a petite 20-gauge B-SS sidelock suddenly appears, and it is quietly suggested that the guest try a more appropriate weapon.

The B-SS sidelock is light and handy, with the 20-gauge guns weighing approximately six pounds and the 12-gauge guns weighing approximately six pounds, six ounces. Those weights vary several ounces if the gun has 28-inch barrels, which by the

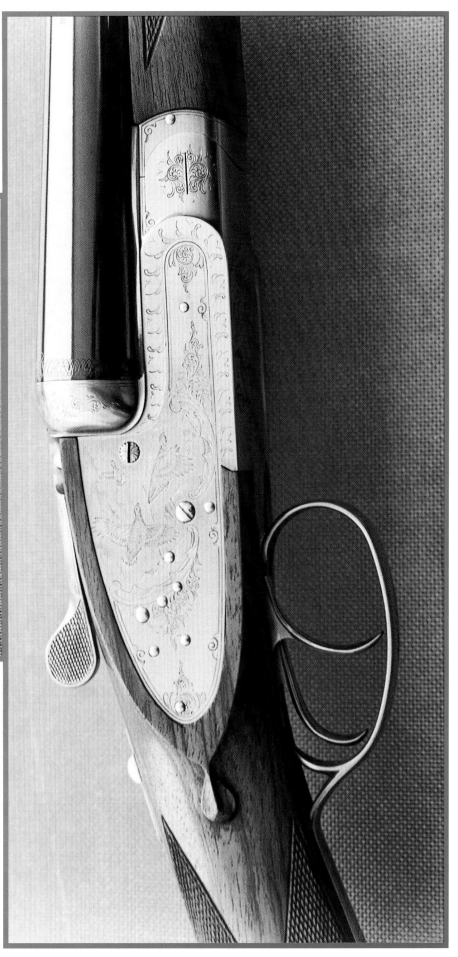

The game-scene version depicts grouse which are realistic and lifelike. The gold-line cocking indicators are found only on game-scene engraved guns.

way, are seen much less frequently then the 26-inch barreled guns. I wonder if when Don Zutz was examining the B-SS sidelock, he wasn't looking at a gun with 28-inch barrels. They seem heftier and came choked modified and full. All of the 26-inch barrel guns came with improved cylinder and modified chokes, and handle like a lethal wand. The 20 gauges—well—they leap to your shoulder, and it doesn't seem like they weigh anything at all.

The real mystery is why they weren't big sellers. Part of it must be timing. In 1983 when the B-SS sidelock was first

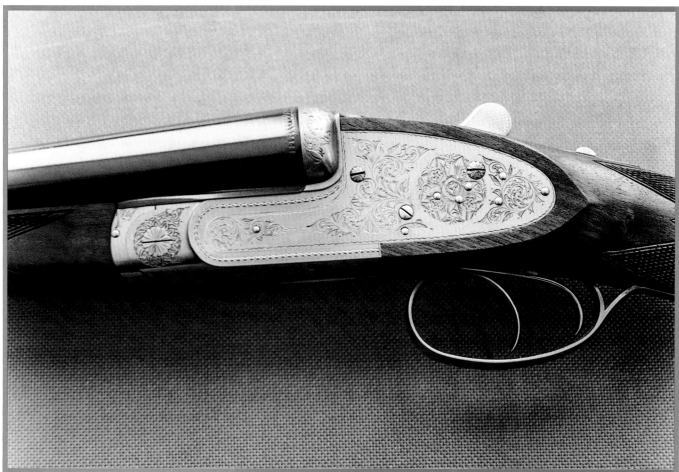

Notice the seven-pin lock mechanism, more engraving on top of frame and down the rib as well. Also note that the "Browning" name is engraved on this rose and scroll version.

introduced, double barrel shotguns were not nearly as popular as they have become in the last several years. Consider the recent revival of the A.H. Fox. Browning must also shoulder some of the blame. It appears as though Browning did not recognize what it had to offer. The owner's manual, for example, was merely a two-page insert in the manual for the B-SS boxlock. A serious marketing effort would have drawn a greater distinction between Browning's sturdy boxlock and its birdy sidelock. Whatever the reason, it is a shame that so few of the sidelocks were made.

If you have the good fortune to own one, you already know it is Browning's best gun. If you can find one, grab it quickly. This best won't get better, just increasingly scarce.

A special thanks to the owners of the B-SS sidelocks illustrated in this article, and to Buck Hamlin and Kirk Merrington for sharing their knowledge and expertise.

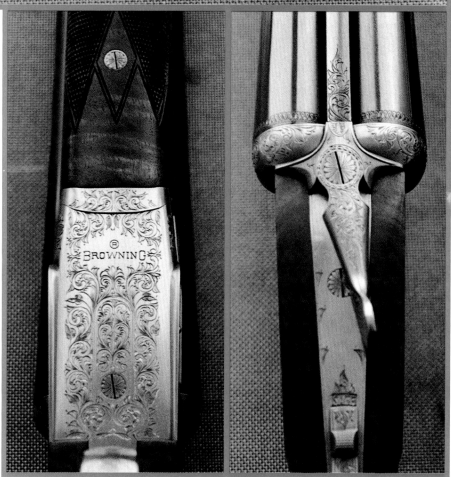

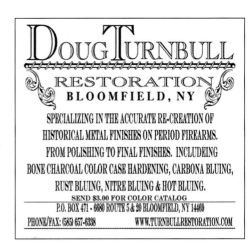

An Introduction To Antique
English Cartridge Loading Tools

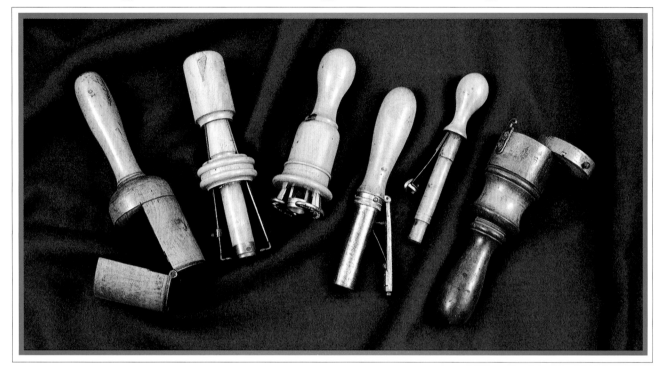

by Andrew Iosson
Photography by Chris Walker

Following the introduction of the breechloader into general usage during the second half of the nineteenth century, the progressive sportsman had to adapt from loading the gun directly with percussion caps, powder, wads and shot to using a self-contained cartridge.

The development of the pinfire breech-loading shotgun and rifle originated in France and was only generally introduced to Britain at the *Great Exhibition* at Crystal Palace, London, in 1851. Shortly after this, the pinfire breechloader was embraced by Joseph Lang Gunmaker of London and others who started to manufacture their own versions in England during the 1850s.

Factory-loaded shells were not readily available in many parts of the world and there was probably a mistrust of factory-loaded ammunition combined with a desire by the more traditional sportsmen to continue to load the gun themselves. During the nineteenth century the newfangled cartridges were relatively expensive in comparison to the price of loose powder and shot or indeed the cost of a shotgun. As late as 1899 Eley Brothers of London were selling a box of one hundred 12-gauge-loaded shot shells for 10 shillings (80 U.S. cents at today's exchange rate) compared to the new cost of a cheap shotgun in 1899 at £3.00 (U.S. $4.90). The introduction of the breechloader therefore generated a new demand amongst many sportsmen to reload the cartridges after use.

The earliest English pinfire guns and rifles were often cased with French loading tools usually made from box-wood which is a very tight-grained strong yellow or honey-colored hardwood.

English gunmakers were quick to recognize this potential new market for cartridge-loading tools and patents were filed by several of them for tools to load pinfire cartridges as early as the late 1850s. Charles Lancaster, gunmaker of London, filed patent No. 1361 in 16 June 1858, which consisted of a bench-mounted machine to fill the shot shell and close the end of the case onto a top wad. G. Jeffries, Gunmaker of Norwich, followed with patent No. 4164 in 13 April 1859. Another famous English gunmaker to register one of the early patents was J. Purdey under patent No. 302 in 5 February 1861.

These early tools were all very large and robust and although well made have an almost crude appearance in comparison to the sophistication employed in later tools of the late pinfire to early centerfire period.

All of the earliest patents and loading tools manufactured related to loading pinfire cartridges. Pinfire cases have very little rim on the shell head and therefore the tools relied upon the pin protruding from the head of the shell to grip and hold the cartridge case to stop it revolving when producing the rolled turnover at the mouth of the case. Many

French loading tools, from left, are for decapping and recapping pinfire shot shells, trimming the case, ramming the wads and producing the rolled closure. These types of tools would have been in use in the 1850–1860 period.

of these tools were not suitable for loading centerfire ammunition as, due to their design, there would have been a danger of detonating the center primer when loading. Consequently the introduction of the centerfire cartridge in the early 1860s which had no external pin but a large rim on the brass shell head, meant that new designs of loading tools were required which gripped the brass rim of the shell to prevent this turning when the rolled turnover closure was created at the mouth of the case, thereby avoiding contact with the center primer. Further designs were patented for both dual function which could be used for pinfire or centerfire ammunition and, subsequently, with the obsolescence of the pinfire, solely for use with centerfire ammunition.

It is sometimes difficult to accurately date production of many of the individual tools to specific years as there was considerable overlap in their manufacture and use, but as you can see from these developments, as a general guide, the earliest tools were suitable for loading pinfire shells only (approximately 1851 to 1880s, followed by a transitional period in which tools could be used for either pinfire or centerfire, approximately 1861 to 1900, followed by centerfire tools only, 1870s to the present day).

Details of the G. Jeffries 1859 patent cast in the side of the tool can be seen above. Below: A close-up of the G. Jeffries badge.

Sheffield in the north of England, which is my home town, had a long tradition in the metal and plate industry with many factories already having expertise in the manufacture of powder and shot flasks and other muzzleloading gun accessories. Several of these Sheffield-based companies quickly adapted to designing and producing new cartridge-loading tools. You may be familiar with names such as James Dixon & Sons (trademark—a bugle or trumpet), G. & J. W. Hawksley, and William Bartram and Company (trademark "nimrod" with a riding hat and crop), all of whom began to patent and produce their own loading tools as early as the 1860s, which were exported throughout the world.

Tools were made to decap the fired shell case, recap, trim the case to the desired length, measure the powder and shot charges, ram the wads, and produce the rolled crimp or turnover. Full brass cases required a different set of tools to close the brass ends of the shells. They ranged from the simple and practical to the extremely complex and typified Victorian innovation and eccentricity at its best.

The tools were produced by each maker in a variety of qualities ranging from "best" which was invariably made of solid nickel or as the catalogues describe it "British Plate" and of very high quality finish, down through lacquered polished brass with color case-hardened steel levers to the more basic japanned (painted) version, which in turn was produced in different grades denoted by the color of the japanning. Materials for making handles ranged from maple or beech, which was "ebonized" (painted black) on the lower-priced tools, through boxwood, rosewood, and ebony to black buffalo horn. Ivory was occasionally used on special-order sets which often also had the metal fittings gold plated. Such elaborate sets of tools may sometimes be seen cased with the "Best" London guns which were supplied by special order to the Indian nobility in the nineteenth century.

During the nineteenth century and early years of the twentieth century many British sportsmen traveled to Africa and Asia in the quest of big game, taking with them their English-made breech-loading rifles. It was frequently necessary to reload ammunition "in the field" and double rifles were often sold cased with the necessary tools to decap and recap the shell case, cast and swage the bullet, measure powder charges, and seat the bullet in the case. Sometimes these tools can be found stamped or engraved with the number of the rifle and the gunmaker's or manufacturer's name or initials, but more frequently they will only show the caliber. Tools for loading rifle cartridges are always of high-quality manufacture and due to their scarcity are now highly desirable.

James Dixon & Sons of Cornish Place, Sheffield, England, was perhaps the most prolific manufacturer and the company always stamped its tools with its catalogue pattern number thus identifying particular patterns, presumably for ease of reordering. They produced a series of catalogues of the loading tools, of which I have seen examples from 1879 through to the 1920s. By the 1905 catalogue, the range of gun accessories and loading tools listed had greatly reduced to a couple of pages only and by World War I the manufacture of shooting accessories had probably ceased. Although later tools marked with the James Dixon & Sons' name, or simply JD&S, are encountered. From their appearance, these tools are of inferior quality and were probably made by other manufacturers and only retailed by James Dixon & Sons. A copy of the company's 1883 catalogue (probably its heyday of manufacture of gun implements) was reprinted by Ken Trotman in 1984 and contains illustrations of Dixon's range of gun accessories and loading tools with the relevant catalogue pattern numbers and original prices per dozen.

G. & J.W. Hawksley of Carver Works, Carver Street, Sheffield, also produced catalogues on their range of loading tools and gun accessories. The earliest catalogue I have recorded is 1889, but although this shows catalogue numbers alongside each of the tools, unlike the James Dixon range these catalogue numbers were not stamped on the actual tools.

Lightwood tools can usually be recognized by a partridge (the company's trademark) stamped on the lever and occasionally "L&S". Again a range of tools in different qualities was produced to suit the pocket of the customer.

Henry Arthur Ward was a gunmaker at Russell Street, Birmingham. The company's tools are often unmarked, but occasionally will be found stamped "Ward". Generally the

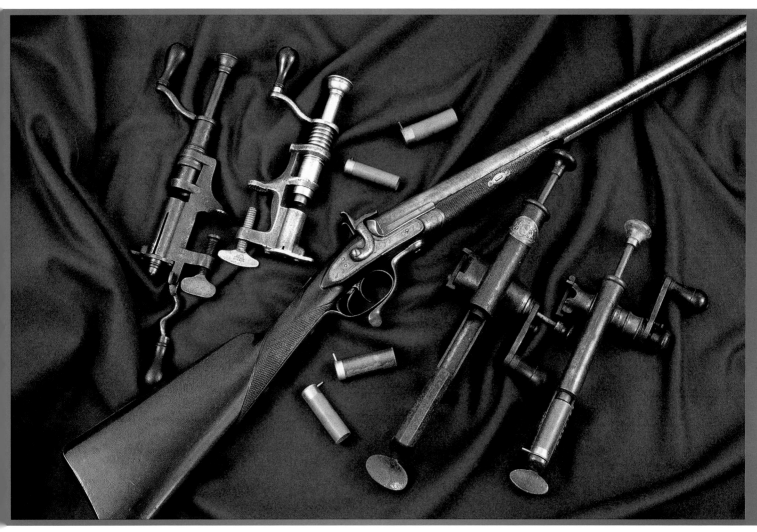

A selection of very early bench-mounted loading tools manufactured during the period 1859–1865. Makers include, from left: G. Jefferies 1859 patent roll crimping tool (16 inches high), G. Jeffries patent 6 August 1860, and two early tools by W. Bartram, Sheffield.

William Bartram & Company also of Sheffield produced large numbers of gun accessories and loading tools, but ceased trading in the 1880s, and I have never seen a catalogue produced by them. Their tools usually are stamped with their name and trademark and although they follow the general pattern of Dixon and Hawksley, their tools were often a little more decorative, or stylistic.

Following what must have been the success of the Sheffield manufacturers in selling the new breech-loading tools, other English manufacturers started to patent, produce, and market their own tools. Birmingham had long been a center of gunmaking in England and Lightwood & Son and H.A. Ward & Sons, both of Birmingham, patented several designs in the 1880s and produced a variety of tools.

tools I have inspected are late 19th century or early 20th century and not of the quality of the tools produced by the Sheffield manufacturers.

A well-established London engineering firm, John Greenfield, who had a background of manufacturing tools for the gunmaker and high-quality bullet molds, also made a limited number of cartridge loading tools. All are extremely well made, robust, marked either "Greenfield London" or "JG" and are of a distinctive design differing significantly from the style used by other makers.

In addition many gunmakers commissioned Dixon, Hawksley, or one of the other makers of accessories, to produce a range of tools stamped with the gunmaker's name for retail by the gunmaker, either as part of a cased gun set or

to be sold separately. The P. Webley & Son catalogue for 1888 shows a wide range of tools with catalogue numbers. I have seen examples of their tools which are all stamped with the catalogue number, but not their name. I have also seen tools marked with the names of the following gunmakers: Alexander Henry of Edinburgh, G.W. Ingram of Glasgow, W. Pape of Newcastle, J. Purdey & Sons of London, Isaac Hollis and Midland Gun Company of Birmingham, although it is doubtful if any of these gunmakers actually manufactured the tools, but simply acted as retailers.

sories cased with them. Breechloaders sold in oak or leather cases were often accompanied by a set of loading tools designed to fit comfortably and flat in the case compartments. A few of these tools were bench mounted, but the majority were designed to be hand held as they were smaller and took up less room in the case.

Powder and shot measures whilst performing a relatively basic function can be found in a huge variety, both in size and complexity of operation, using triggers, levers and shut-offs to accurately fill the shell with the correct charge.

Some examples of tools manufactured for the loading of rifle cartridges.
Below: The range in quality of Horsley's patent recapping tools, manufactured by James Dixon (catalogue No. 1181) from the "Best" on the left (with nickel tubes and brightly blued fittings at a cost of £102 per dozen) to the medium-quality (lacquered brass tubes and blued steel lever at £78 per dozen) and the common quality (brass tubes with all steel parts japanned at a cost of £60 per dozen) on the right.

Cased English guns had always been sold with the necessary accessories for loading, including powder and shot flasks, wad cutters, cappers, etc., and it would be expected therefore that the new breechloaders should also have the relevant acces-

Following the introduction of bulk smokeless powders, new measures were required and many were designed for use with several types of powder with scales marked for black powder, E.C., and Schultz.

During the later years of the nineteenth century and

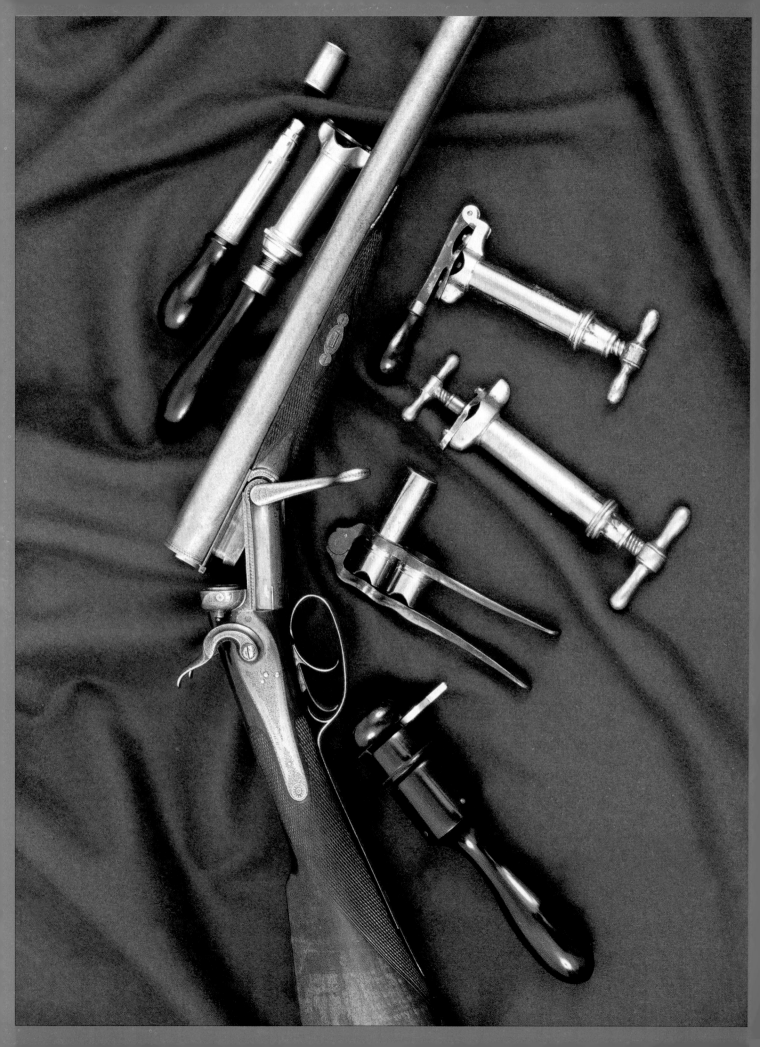

into the twentieth century many gun-makers and dealers bought primed cases from cartridge manufacturers such as Eley of London or Kynoch of Birmingham that had the gunmaker's or dealer's name printed on the case and they loaded the cases to sell as their own make. There was a range of tools produced for "shop" use, i.e., for bulk loading by these gunmakers or dealers and the tools can be recognized by their larger and more robust construction. The largest of these machines was "The Climax" patented in 1887 and manufactured by James Dixon & Sons who amazingly offered these for sale up to the 1960s. It utilized one hundred shot-shell cases for filling and wadding.

Large-scale production of hand-loading tools appears to have stopped by the early twentieth century, presumably with the increase in reliability and reduction in the price of factory-loaded ammunition. Gunmakers' catalogues of the 1920s only show a very limited range of tools, and production of the expensive "best" quality and more innovative tools had ceased. From examination of a large number of different tools,

Above, from left: 10-gauge bullet swager, 12-gauge decapper and recapper, and a 12-gauge creaser which is used to crimp the brass case onto the lead bullet.
Below: James Dixon & Sons "Best Quality" British plate tools.
Facing page: Loading tools made for cased guns. As can be seen from the selection, all are of high quality with great attention to polishing, lacquer and bluing.

it is clear that in the later period of manufacture after say 1900, the manufacturers were outsourcing more components from the same sub-contract manufacturers rather than making all the parts "in house" and the quality and finish on the tools is poorer.

The roll turnover closure was superceded by the star crimp and the vast majority of tools have now become collectors' prized pieces or are gathering dust somewhere in gun shops, homes, and barns.

The James Dixon factory in Cornish Place, Sheffield, a large Georgian brick building constructed in a quadrangle with a central courtyard, adjacent to the River Don, still exists, but is now converted to a luxury apartment block. All of the once-famous names in gun tool manufacture have long since ceased trading, but their names live on in gun cases all over the world.

To date little has been published about antique English gun tools and in-depth knowledge of the subject is limited to a few established collectors, with help from old gunmakers' catalogues and patent records. Gun tools are still frequently seen for sale at auctions, arms fairs, and antique markets, often completely wrongly described and, where the seller is ignorant of the rarity or use of the tool, bargains still exist.

In future articles I hope to deal in more detail with some of the patents, makers, and types of tools, in order to help the reader grade and date the various tools, learn more about the manufacturers, and recognize the rare and more exotic items.

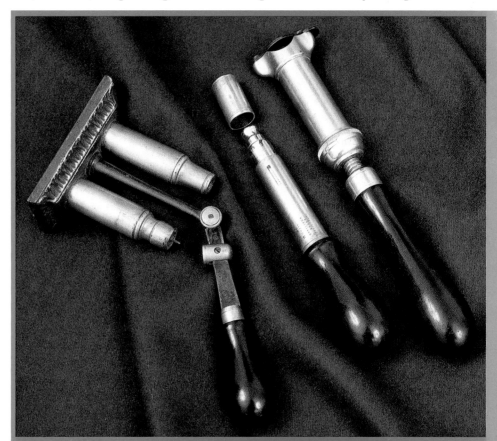

L.C. SMITH
(Marlin) 12 ga., "Deluxe F. Gr.," sidelock, 28" Simmons VR bbls., BT and deluxe walnut, one of only 188. 100% new, never fired $1850

WM. DOUGLAS & SON
28 ga., "Small Bore," SxS boxlock, 27" bbls., AE, SST, str. stock with Ck. butt, new-in-maker's case $4800
Vern - 336-998-2806

FRANCOTTE
12 ga. high grade 2-3/4", ejector 28" straight stock. Super nice $2500

W.C. SCOTT & SON
High grade, 10 gauge Damascus hammer gun, straight stock, 28", gorgeous.......$2500

PARKER
PH, 16 gauge twist barrel 30". Very good.................................$1250
John - 817-335-3005 days, 817-249-6601 eves.

W. RICHARDS
12 B hammer gun, DT, 28" rebrowned Damascus bbls., refinished stock with 14-1/2" LOP, fitted with Briley 20 ga. tube set $1150
Doug - 713-840-1155

W.&C. SCOTT
12 ga., 30" IC/IM, sidelock, clips, crossbolt, SG $3995

ITHACA
4E, SxS, 32", Flues, reconditioned like new.................................$2850

P. BERNARDELLI
12 ga., sidelock, light engraving with gold animals, 27-1/2" $2500

HOLLAND & HOLLAND
Double rifle, 10 ga., cased with acc., HMR, UL, reconditioned........................$22,000

AYA
No. 2, 16 ga., 28" IC/M, 14-3/4" LOP, CB, SG......................................$2750
No. 2, 28/.410 combo, round action, upgraded wood, cased................................$6000

RICHLAND (ERBI)
28 ga., 26" IC/M, PG, BT, Ext., 13-1/2" LOP $950
Norm - 906-875-3119

POWELL
2" 12 bore, 27" DT, 5 lb. 7 oz., cased.................................$7500

WESTLEY RICHARDS
12 bore, 27", DT, gold name $6500

BOSWELL
2-1/2" 12 bore, Damascus, DT, game scenes, cased $9500

DICKSON
Round action, 2-1/2" 12 bore, 28", DT, cased $21,000
Mark - 928-525-1794

HEER KERRATH SUHL
20 ga., 10 M/M? Cape gun $1000
Chuck - 417-718-5400

ARRIETA
M-803, 12 ga., 28" barrels, 2-3/4", lengthened forcing cones, DT, SG, maker's case .$1600

BROWNING BSS
12 ga., 28" barrels, ST, SG LOP 14.8".................................$500

FRENCH LIGHT GAME GUN
12 ga. 28" barrels, DT, SG, LOP 14.5", 2-3/4"..............................$500

MANTON
28 ga., 28" barrels, DT, SG, LOP 15", boxlock..............................$4000
Entire collection...$6000
Troop - 503-368-7099

FOX A/E
12 ga., 30", M/F, PG, SF, DT, Krupp..........................$3900
Pat - 719-687-8060

CHARLES HELLIS
2" 12 bore, 26" IC&M, SS, SF, DT, 14-1/4" LOP to checkered butt, cased, excellent $5250

RENATO GAMBA
Princepessa, 28 ga., DT, EJ, SS, SF, LOP to thin pad, SKT & IC, excellent $2550

J.P. SAUER
20 ga., Fortuna, DT, SS, SF, EJT., 26" IC&M, no swivels or cheekpiece. LOP to black pad. Excellent $2695
Bob - 317-842-0927 - leave message

PARKER
PH 16 ga., 28" twist, excellent, original, some case $2750
GH 20 ga., 26" Damascus, very good, original, trace case $3450
Lifter 12 ga., Damascus, good, original, barrel bulge repairable $950

W&C SCOTT
10 ga. hammer, Damascus, beautiful wood, shooter, stunning...........................$3250
Percussion hammer gun, shoots very well. 10/11 gauge..............................$2450
Hans - 509-536-1617 day - 509-922-7815 evenings

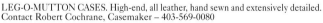

IN APPRECIATION
OUR ADVERTISERS

If you are just interested, or planning to purchase, please give our reputable advertisers a call.
Please tell them you saw it in *The Double Gun Journal!*

If you are interested in advertising in *The Double Gun Journal* please contact us for more information:

U.S.A. & All Other Countries

Valerie J. Raba
101 East 7th Street
Frederick, Maryland
21701
U.S.A.

Tel. 301-694-5001
Fax 301-694-5212

Daniel Philip Côté
Post Office Box 550
East Jordan, Michigan
49727-9636
U.S.A.

Tel. 231-536-7439
Fax 231-536-7450

U. K. & Northern Europe

Tony Barrett
Feldon House
Banbury Street
Kineton
Warwickshire CV350JS
England

Tel. 011•44•1926•641640
Fax 011•44•1926•641595

Book design by Daniel Philip Côté, Publisher • Typeset by Kay Seelye, Boyne City, Michigan
Address Changes and Other Subscription Queries please call 231-536-7439
To place an order or to inquire about contributing material for publication, call 1-800-447-1658